THE SWEET POTATO QUEENS

BIG-ASS COMPENDIUM OF

FAT & HAPPY:

Recipes to Improve Your Disposition

JILL CONNER BROWNE

SHELTON HOUSE PRESS

ALSO BY JILL CONNER BROWNE

Fat Is the New 30:
The Sweet Potato Queens' Guide to Coping with (the crappy parts of) Life

American Thighs:
The Sweet Potato Queens' Guide to Preserving Your Assets

The Sweet Potato Queens' Guide to Raising Children for Fun and Profit

The Sweet Potato Queens' First Big-Ass Novel:
Stuff We Didn't Actually Do, but Could Have, and May Yet
(With Karin Gillespie)

The Sweet Potato Queens' Wedding Planner/Divorce Guide

The Sweet Potato Queens' Field Guide to Men:
Every Man I Love is Either Married, Gay, or Dead

The Sweet Potato Queens' Big-Ass Cookbook
(and Financial Planner)

God Save the Sweet Potato Queens

The Sweet Potato Queens' Book of Love

The Sweet Potato Queens'
BIG-ASS COMPENDIUM OF FAT & HAPPY

The Sweet Potato Queens' Big-Ass Compendium of Fat & Happy:
Recipes to Improve Your Disposition
by
Jill Conner Browne

Published by
Shelton House Press, LLC.
561 West Main Street
Raymond, MS 39154
info@sheltonhousepress.com

Cover design by Steve Erickson at The Cirlot Agency. Book design by Kyle Jennings

First Edition 2022

Library of Congress Control Number:
2021907031

ISBN: 978-1-7370265-0-1 (PB)

Manufactured in the United States of America

WARNING AND HOLD HARMLESS: ALL OF THE RECIPES HEREIN ARE POISON! IF YOU EAT THIS STUFF ALL THE TIME, YOU WILL DIE – AND YOU WILL DIE WITH A HUGE BEE-HIND; HOWEVER, THEY ARE VERY GOOD FOR YOUR DISPOSITION. *PROCEED AT YOUR OWN RISK.* BY SO DOING, YOU AND YOUR HEIRS AND ASSIGNS AGREE TO HOLD HARMLESS THE AUTHOR, PUBLISHER, SPQ, INC., SWEET POTATO QUEENS' WEBSITE, LLC., AND THEIR RESPECTIVE PARENTS, SUBSIDIARIES, AND AFFILIATE COMPANIES, EMPLOYEES, CONTRACTORS, AGENTS, SUPPLIERS, DISTRIBUTORS, AND ADVERTISING/PROMOTION AGENCIES, AS WELL AS EACH SUCH COMPANIES' OWNERS, OFFICERS, DIRECTORS, EMPLOYEES, CONTRACTORS, AND AGENTS FROM AND AGAINST ANY CLAIM OR CAUSE OF ACTION, INCLUDING, BUT NOT LIMITED TO, PERSONAL INJURY, DEATH, OR DAMAGE TO OR LOSS OF PROPERTY OR PROFIT, ARISING OUT OF USE OR MISUSE OF ANY INFORMATION, INGREDIENTS, DIRECTIONS, OR RECIPE HEREIN.

LIMITS OF LIABILITY AND DISCLAIMER OF WARRANTY: THE AUTHOR AND PUBLISHER OF THIS BOOK, SPQ, INC., AND SWEET POTATO QUEENS WEBSITE, LLC. HAVE USED THEIR BEST EFFORTS IN PREPARING THIS MATERIAL. THE AUTHOR AND PUBLISHER MAKE NO REPRESENTATIONS OR WARRANTIES WITH RESPECT TO THE ACCURACY, APPLICABILITY, FITNESS OR COMPLETENESS OF THE CONTENTS OF THIS MATERIAL. THEY DISCLAIM ANY WARRANTIES EXPRESSED OR IMPLIED, MERCHANTABILITY, OR FITNESS FOR ANY PARTICULAR PURPOSE. THE AUTHOR AND PUBLISHER SHALL IN NO EVENT BE HELD LIABLE FOR ANY LOSS OR OTHER DAMAGES, INCLUDING BUT NOT LIMITED TO, SPECIAL, INCIDENTAL, CONSEQUENTIAL, OR OTHER DAMAGES. THIS MATERIAL CONTAINS ELEMENTS PROTECTED UNDER INTERNATIONAL AND FEDERAL COPYRIGHT AND TRADEMARK LAWS AND TREATIES. ANY UNAUTHORIZED REPRINT OR USE OF THIS MATERIAL IS PROHIBITED.

NOTE REGARDING FOOD ALLERGIES: I, JILL CONNER BROWNE, THE AUTHOR OF THIS WORK, PERSONALLY, DO NOT HAVE ANY FOOD ALLERGIES; THEREFORE, I HAVE NOT MADE ANY INGREDIENT ADJUSTMENTS, ALTERNATIVE RECOMMENDATIONS, OR CONSIDERATION WHATSOEVER FOR SUCH IN THIS MATERIAL. IF YOU HAVE FOOD ALLERGIES OR YOU ARE PREPARING FOOD FOR SOMEONE WHO DOES OR MIGHT HAVE FOOD ALLERGIES, THEN IT IS YOUR PERSONAL RESPONSIBILITY TO TAKE THE APPROPRIATE STEPS. READ, FOLLOW, AND ABIDE BY PRODUCT LABELS AND WARNINGS. *BE PARTICULAR!*

THE SWEET POTATO QUEENS'

BIG-ASS COMPENDIUM OF

FAT & HAPPY:

Recipes to Improve Your Disposition

TABLE OF CONTENTS

(Continued on the next page.)

DEDICATION

All versions of this book must be dedicated, along with all my love and gratitude, to the one person who has quite literally slaved for, again quite literally, years over the endless, mind-numbing details required to produce what, on the surface, appears to be such a simple set of documents. He is the one for whom it is my joy and privilege to cook all this stuff and who eats everything I put in front of him with effusive dee-light: my very own husband, The Cutest Boy in the World, Kyle Jennings.

And, many thanks to all of you in the Queendom who have shared so many great recipes with me over the years. Keep 'em coming! We gotta EAT!

There Are NO Funny Stories in This Book.

There is food and only food. The purpose of this *Big-Ass Compendium* of recipes (and only recipes) is at least two-fold.

First-fold: (and don't presume for an instant that this is The Most Important Thing because it so is Not) is to give YOU death-defying recipes from ALL of the Sweet Potato Queens® books (so far) in one convenient pile. These are recipes that I have already not ONLY put into handy-dandy physical books for your absolute dee-light and convenience, I have additionally, on far too many occasions, E-MAILED THEM, individually and personally, to hundreds and hundreds of y'all over the last 20-odd years, to the utter ruination of my disposition. And so now, I purport to give those to you in plain ole bald-faced recipe format with absolutely no entertaining embellishments whatsoever.

Second-fold: (and assuming that you do know me, you also know THIS is actually The Most Important Thing) is to PREVENT you from e-mailing and Facebooking and Tweeting me that you "lost/loaned/gave away your book(s)" and you "MUST HAVE CHOCOLATE STUFF (or Whatever It Is You're Currently Craving) RIGHT THIS VERY SECOND OR YOU WILL SURELY DIE" and would I please take the time out of MY day to go personally find which book of the NINE that your desired recipe is in (oddly enough, I do not know them all by heart) and would I furthermore then take the time out of MY day to sit down and RE-TYPE said recipe FOR YOU— when AS WE ALL KNOW, I have ALREADY DONE THAT when I put them ALL into convenient BOOKS for you—but which YOU have somehow—through no fault or responsibility of MINE—not managed to hold onto. I mean, I love y'all to bits and all that but I never intended to take y'all to raise.

Additional-fold: At the bottom of each recipe, you will see the title of the book it came from. (In the e-book version of this *Big-Ass Compendium*, those are user-friendly LINKS to the electronic version where you can easily and immediately purchase it and also buy MORE print editions of each book for physically sharing with the poor Uninitiated out there.

If you ARE the Uninitiated, you will have all the info you need for getting ALL NINE of the Sweet Potato Queens® books and reading them yourownself or you can listen to me read to you, not just the recipes but also the hilarious stories surrounding all of them...except the new ones, of course. (See "One More-Fold" below.)

Also in the electronic version of this book, you will find LINKS to some ingredients and pots, pans, bowls, utensils, etc. that you might be lacking. Where available I personally use and therein source USA made or assembled items. Some of the LINKS that appear throughout the recipes are compiled in the Recommendations section at the end of this book.

One More-Fold: I have also included 33 NEW recipes that will appear in the next SPQ™ book as well—just to demonstrate what a Good Sport I am.

My hope—no, my prayer—is that y'all will also buy the printed copies and their electronic twins of all nine of my other books, and the audio versions of them as well BECAUSE I have, once again, *massive* plastic surgery needs and your purchases are simple ways that YOU can help!

You can download the Kindle App and the electronic version of this book can come straight to your cell phone or tablet so you can easily shop for the ingredients of your favorite SPQ™ recipes AND you're not likely to be loaning out your PHONE, tablet, or Kindle then e-mailing me in tears for some recipe. By owning this printed version, you don't have to worry about spilling bacon grease on your phone while you're cooking. And with the audio versions of my other books, you can have me "in your ear" while you're lollygagging, cooking, walking, or driving—how great is that?

As always, remember: *These recipes are poison!* If you eat this food all of the time, you will die (sooner rather than later) and you will die with a HUGE ASS. However, taken in as much moderation as one can muster, they are GOOD for your DISPOSITION; therefore, they are my contribution to World Peace. You are welcome!

Basic Stuff to Know Before You
Begin Using These Recipes

👑 WHENEVER a recipe calls for "vanilla," I will ALWAYS specify that the teaspoon(s) should be "running over." My Mama taught me that rule; it has served me well and will do the same for you, if you mind me.

👑 Unless it is otherwise specified, ANY butter called for herein should be "salted." And you will not find it otherwise.

👑 Likewise, "brown" sugar will nearly always be "dark." I know of only two recipes in here that actually call for the "*LIGHT* brown" variety.

👑 ALL Dark Brown Sugars are NOT created equal and it MATTERS. Compare the brands sold in clear plastic bags and use ONLY the DARKEST available. More expensive does NOT necessarily mean better.

If the recipe does not specifically state the size/type pan to be used, it doesn't really matter. Look at how much is in the bowl and figure out which pan you have that will hold it. I am going out on a limb and assuming that you have sense enough to NOT try to cram a gallon of something into a quart pan—or try to make a quart of something cover the bottom of a gallon pan. Please tell me that my trust is not misplaced.

I suggest that all of these recipes are like personal pan pizzas and mini-watermelons: intended to SERVE ONE. Sharing is a strictly personal decision and, quite frankly, highly over-rated in my opinion. Parents waste years trying to force their offspring to embrace the concept of "share and share alike," to the utter misery of all concerned and the first thing we ALL do as adults is GET OUR OWN STUFF. Let your conscience (or your pants with zippers) be your Sharing Guide.

Be particular!
Jill Conner Browne

RECIPE GROUPS

Okay, here's a list of all of the recipes organized in the groups as I think of them: Breads, Breakfast, Casseroles, Chicken, Dips & Appetizers, Drinks, Meat, Salads, Sammiches, Seafood, Soups & Stews, Sweets, Veggies, and Weird Shit. Following this Grouping is an Alphabetical List of all of the recipes; so, y'all *should* be able to easily find what you're looking for WITHOUT nagging me for it.

BREADS

1. BACON MONKEY BREAD   p. 38
2. BAILEY'S BANANA BREAD   p. 39
3. BARBARA'S BEAUTIFUL CORNBREAD   p. 40
4. BLESSED BACON BISCUITS   p. 41
5. FATTEN-YOU-RIGHT-UP ROLLS V.1   p. 42
6. FATTEN-YOU-RIGHT-UP ROLLS V.2   p. 43
7. HRH JILL'S HO-MADE BLUEBERRY MUFFINS   p. 44
8. LITTLE JEFFREY'S FAVORITE MUFFINS   p. 45
9. MICHAEL'S MAGICAL SWEET POTATO MUFFINS   p. 46
10. MISSISSIPPI SIN   p. 47
11. MOTHER PAYNE'S PERFECT BISCUITS   p. 48
12. RAY LEE'S TOMATO CORNBREAD   p. 49
13. STINKY BREAD   p. 50
14. SWEET POTATO BISCUITS   p. 51
15. SWEET POTATO (QUEEN) CORNBREAD   p. 52
16. TEXAS CORNBREAD   p. 53
17. THE HOLY MOUND   p. 54
18. THE UBIQUITOUS BISCUIT   p. 55

(BREAKFAST on the next page.)

BREAKFAST

CASSEROLES

(Continues on the next page.)

CHICKEN

(DIPS & APPETIZERS on the next page.)

DIPS & APPETIZERS

(DRINKS on the next page.)

DRINKS

MEAT

(Continues on the next page.)

SALADS

(SAMMICHES on the next page.)

SAMMICHES

SEAFOOD

(SOUPS & STEWS on the next page.)

SOUPS & STEWS

SWEETS

(Continues on the next page.)

(Continues on the next page.)

(Continues on the next page.)

VEGGIES

(Continues on the next page.)

WEIRD SHIT

(ALPHABETICAL LIST of all recipes follows.)

ALPHABETICAL LIST

(Continues on the next page.)

(Continues on the next page.)

(Continues on the next page.)

(Continues on the next page.)

(Continues on the next page.)

(Continues on the next page.)

(Continues on the next page.)

(Continues on the next page.)

(Continues on the next page.)

The Sweet Potato Queens'
BIG-ASS COMPENDIUM OF FAT & HAPPY

BREADS

BACON MONKEY BREAD

1 lb. bacon, cooked and crumbled

½ cup Parmesan

1 small onion, chopped

1 stick salted butter, melted

3 10-oz. cans "whomp" biscuits

Preheat oven to 350°F. Mix together bacon bits, Parmesan, and onion. Cut each biscuit into fourths and dip pieces into butter. Put 1/3 of biscuits into a greased Bundt pan, sprinkle with bacon mixture. Repeat layers, filling pan, ending with biscuits on top. Bake for approx. 40 mins. but watch closely. Allow to rest in pan until slightly cooled before turning out onto platter for serving.

The Sweet Potato Queens' Big-Ass Cookbook (and Financial Planner)
(Three Rivers Press, 2003), p. 262

BAILEY'S BANANA BREAD

½ cup softened or melted salted butter

1 cup sugar

2 running over tsp. vanilla

1½ cups flour

1 tsp. salt

1 tsp. baking soda

3-4 over-ripe bananas, creamed

Preheat oven to 325°F. In large bowl, combine all ingredients then pour into a greased loaf pan and bake for 40-60 mins. Test with toothpick for doneness.

*** There is not an omission here — there actually are *no* eggs in this recipe. ***

This will one day appear in yet another *Sweet Potato Queens® book*, God willing.

Barbara's Beautiful Cornbread

3 cups white cornmeal mix

16 oz. sour cream

1/3 cup oil

4 eggs

2 cups Sharp Cheddar, shredded

1 15-oz. can yellow cream corn

1 4-oz. can chopped green chilis

1 medium onion, chopped fine

Several TBSP chopped jalapeños, fresh or canned, to taste

Salted butter

Put 12-inch iron skillet into oven and preheat to 350°F. Mix all ingredients. Take hot skillet from oven. Put a couple TBSP butter in skillet, allow it to melt (put back into oven, if necessary), spreading it evenly in skillet. Sprinkle small amount of cornmeal in skillet, distributing evenly on bottom and sides. Pour batter into hot, buttered skillet. Bake for approx. 55 mins., but watch closely.

NOTE: This makes EXCELLENT PLAIN cornbread as well.
Just eliminate cheese, corn, chilis, onion, and jalapeños and
reduce time of baking.

Fat Is The New 30:
The Sweet Potato Queens' Guide to Coping with (the crappy parts of) Life
(Amazon Publishing, 2012), p. 139

BLESSED BACON BISCUITS
(Damon Lee Fowler's Recipe; used with permission.)

2 cups soft wheat flour

1 tsp. baking powder

1 tsp. salt

6 TBSP bacon drippings, chilled

½ cup milk

Freshly ground pepper, optional

Preheat oven to 450°F. Sift together flour, baking powder, and salt. Cut in bacon drippings to make pea-sized lumps of dough. Make a "well" in center, pour in milk. Mix ONLY until dough pulls away from sides of bowl and is not crumbly. Add small amount milk, if needed. Turn dough out onto a well-floured surface, pat to ½ inch thick. Grind pepper over dough (optional) and fold dough over in half. Pat flat and pepper again if desired. Pat and fold two more times (additional pepper not recommended). Re-flour board. Roll or pat dough out to ¼ inch thickness. Cut into biscuits, bake on an un-greased cookie sheet until lightly browned, 8-10 mins.

The Sweet Potato Queens' First Big-Ass Novel:
Stuff we didn't actually do, but could have, and may yet
(Simon & Schuster, 2008), p. 287

FATTEN-YOU-RIGHT-UP ROLLS V.1

2 sticks salted butter, melted

2 cups sour cream

2 heaping cups self-rising flour

1 lb. Sharp Cheddar, shredded

Preheat oven to 400°F. Mix all ingredients together. Put into a greased muffin pan and bake until browned.

The Sweet Potato Queens' Wedding Planner and Divorce Guide
(Crown Publishers, 2007), *Divorce Guide* side, p. 111

FATTEN-YOU-RIGHT-UP ROLLS V.2

1 stick salted butter, melted

1 cup sour cream

1 heaping cup self-rising flour

Preheat oven to 400°F. Mix all ingredients together. Bake in a greased mini-muffin pan for approx. 12 mins.

The Sweet Potato Queens' Big-Ass Cookbook (and Financial Planner)
(Three Rivers Press, 2003), p. 80

HRH JILL'S HO-MADE BLUEBERRY MUFFINS

2 cups blueberries
(fresh or frozen, rinsed and drained)

4 cups All Purpose flour

1 cup sugar

6 tsp. baking powder

2 tsp. salt

2 tsp. cinnamon

1 stick salted butter, melted

2 cups milk

2 eggs, beaten

2 running-over tsp. vanilla

1 jar lemon curd

Preheat oven to 425°F. Combine dry ingredients in large bowl. Combine wet ingredients in another bowl then mix into dry ingredients. Don't over-mix. Add blueberries and stir just until evenly distributed in batter. Spoon batter into a greased muffin pan. Put dollop of lemon curd on top of each muffin, swirl slightly. Bake until golden brown. (Time depends on muffin size—works well for Minis or Regular.) Serve with butter and honey or plain.

The Sweet Potato Queens' Big-Ass Cookbook (and Financial Planner)
(Three Rivers Press, 2003), p. 142

LITTLE JEFFREY'S FAVORITE MUFFINS

2 cups softened or melted salted butter

4 cups sugar

4 eggs, beaten

4 cups unsweetened applesauce

6 tsp. cinnamon

4 tsp. allspice

2 tsp. cloves

2 tsp. salt

4 tsp. baking soda

8 cups All Purpose flour

2 cups chopped pecans (optional)

Preheat oven to 350°F. In a large bowl, mix butter, and sugar, add eggs. Add applesauce and spices. Stir in flour, soda, salt, and pecans if using. Mix well. Spoon mixture into a greased, Texas-sized muffin pan or greased mini-muffin pans. Bake approx. 10 mins. for mini-muffins. Adjust times for larger muffins. Makes nearly endless supply of minis. Batter will keep for weeks in refrigerator, nearly forever in freezer.

Baked muffins also freeze well—reheat before serving. May half the recipe if you don't like having something so delicious so handy by. Still makes a lot though.

This will one day appear in yet another *Sweet Potato Queens® book*, God willing.

MICHAEL'S MAGICAL SWEET POTATO MUFFINS

1 cup dark brown sugar

½ cup canola oil

1 running over tsp. vanilla

2 eggs

2 cups flour

2 tsp. baking powder

1 tsp. cinnamon

1 tsp. nutmeg

½ tsp. allspice

½ tsp. salt

2 large sweet potatoes, baked or boiled,
peeled & mashed (may use canned)

½ cup raisins (optional)

1 cup pecan pieces (optional)

Preheat oven to 350°F. In a bowl, whisk together sugar, oil, vanilla, and eggs. In another bowl, combine dry ingredients. Add sweet potatoes to dry ingredients then stir in sugar mixture. (If desired, add ½ cup raisins and/or 1 cup pecan pieces.) Stir only until fully mixed. Bake in a greased muffin pan for 25-30 mins.

American Thighs:
The Sweet Potato Queens' Guide to Preserving Your Assets
(Simon & Schuster, 2009), p. 298

MISSISSIPPI SIN

1 loaf *good* French bread

1½ cups sour cream

2 cups Sharp Cheddar cheese, shredded

1 8-oz. pkg. cream cheese

1/3 cup chopped green chilis

1/3 cup green onions, chopped

Bread chunks or tortilla chips

Preheat oven to 350°F. Slice top off bread and reserve. Carve out middle of bread, cutting into chunks for dipping. Combine sour cream, cheese, cream cheese, chilis, and green onions. Stuff mixture into bread shell. Replace top and wrap entire loaf in *HEAVY* aluminum foil. Bake 1 hour. Serve with bread chunks and/or tortilla chips.

The Sweet Potato Queens' Wedding Planner and Divorce Guide
(Crown Publishers, 2007), *Wedding Planner* side, p. 82

Mother Payne's Perfect Biscuits

1 cup buttermilk

1 heaping TBSP Crisco® shortening

Self-rising flour

Salted butter, softened

Preheat oven to 425°F. In a large bowl, pour buttermilk and add Crisco®. Stir in self-rising flour until it makes crumbly dough. Spread towel on counter and sprinkle liberally with flour. Put dough on towel and pat out to approx. ¼ to ½ inch thickness. (Don't overwork dough.) Cut into biscuits. (These will be lumpy.) Dip back of teaspoon into butter and put a dot on top of each biscuit. Bake on a greased cookie sheet until light golden brown.

Fat Is The New 30:
The Sweet Potato Queens' Guide to Coping with (the crappy parts of) Life
(Amazon Publishing, 2012), p. 136

RAY LEE'S TOMATO CORNBREAD

1 pan *real* cornbread (not Jiffy®)

1 can chicken broth (may need slightly more)

1 cup green onions (chopped, with tops)

1 tsp. black pepper

1 TBSP sugar

3 heaping TBSP salted butter, melted

2½ to 3 cups very ripe tomatoes, peeled & chopped
(may use canned, if necessary)

Preheat oven to 350°F. In a large bowl, crumble cornbread and mix with all other ingredients. (Add enough broth to make it moist, not soupy.) Put into a greased pan and bake until set in center and brown on top. (Finished product will be more like dressing or stuffing than cornbread.)

The Sweet Potato Queens' Big-Ass Cookbook (and Financial Planner)
(Three Rivers Press, 2003), p. 19

STINKY BREAD

1 loaf *good* French bread

1 cup salted butter, softened

1 or 2 cloves garlic

1¼ TBSP dried basil (crushed)

2 TBSP capers, rinsed, drained, minced

1 lb. sliced mozzarella cheese

Salt to taste

With a bread knife, cut off the top and sides of the bread but leave bottom intact. Put bread on large sheet of *HEAVY* aluminum foil on a cookie sheet. Slice bread almost through at approx. 1-inch intervals and put a slice of mozzarella in each slot. Mix together butter, garlic, basil, and capers. "Ice" the top and sides of bread with the mixture. Shape foil into a "cradle" around bread. Put in oven on "broil" until brown and gooey. (If cheese is not melted completely, switch oven to bake for a few minutes until it is.)

The Sweet Potato Queens' Big-Ass Cookbook (and Financial Planner)
(Three Rivers Press, 2003), p. 44

SWEET POTATO BISCUITS

5 medium-size sweet potatoes, boiled, peeled, & mashed

3 to 5 cups sugar

4 to 5 cups self-rising flour

2 cups shortening (or salted butter)

1 to 2 cups buttermilk

Preheat oven to 400°F. Mix sugar into mashed sweet potatoes to taste. Make biscuits — using self-rising flour, shortening and buttermilk. Gently mix in sweet potatoes — don't over-work the dough. If the dough is too wet, add flour. Too dry, add buttermilk. These can be patted out and cut into biscuits or dropped. (Makes a TON — uncooked dough freezes great.) If you are going to "pat them out," you need to do it on a well-floured surface then pat or roll out to ½-inch thickness and cut biscuits; if "dropped" then not. Bake on an un-greased pan to desired brownness.

The Sweet Potato Queens' Big-Ass Cookbook (and Financial Planner)
(Three Rivers Press, 2003), p. 140

SWEET POTATO (QUEEN) CORNBREAD

1 cup All Purpose flour

1 cup yellow cornmeal

4 tsp. baking powder

1 tsp. salt

½ cup sugar

6 TBSP milk

3 medium sweet potatoes, cooked, peeled, & mashed
(Substitute: 1 16-oz. can sweet potatoes)

2 large eggs

3 TBSP oil

Preheat oven to 425°F. Mix dry ingredients in one bowl, wet ingredients in another—then combine, stirring just until moist. Put into a greased muffin pan. Bake approx. 15-20 mins.

The Sweet Potato Queens' Big-Ass Cookbook (and Financial Planner)
(Three Rivers Press, 2003), p. 28

TEXAS CORNBREAD

1 cup plain flour

1 cup self-rising flour

1 packed cup *LIGHT* brown sugar

1 cup white sugar

4 eggs

1 cup canola oil

2 cups chopped pecans

1 running-over tsp. vanilla

Preheat oven to 350°F. Mix all ingredients and pour into a greased 10" x 14" (deep sides) pan. (Size matters!) Bake for 20-25 mins.

Do NOT overcook. Should be slightly chewy.

IF you decide to share, don't use your good pan as it will *never* be returned; use disposable ones.

American Thighs:
The Sweet Potato Queens' Guide to Preserving Your Assets
(Simon & Schuster, 2009), p. 299

THE HOLY MOUND

1 can crescent rolls

1 lb. bacon, cooked and crumbled

1 lb. smoked gouda (or other smoked cheese), grated

1 cup dark brown sugar

1 cup chopped pecan

Preheat oven to 375°F. Unroll crescent rolls and lay out in two (2) 4-sheet rectangles on an un-greased cookie sheet. Top each rectangle with as much bacon, cheese, and pecans as possible. Cover rectangles with remaining dough and pinch edges together to form "package." Bake until brown. Cut into wedges to serve. Can be prepared in advance, covered in plastic wrap and refrigerated until baking.

The Sweet Potato Queens' Wedding Planner and Divorce Guide
(Crown Publishers, 2007), *Divorce Guide* side, p. 112

THE UBIQUITOUS BISCUIT

3 cups All Purpose flour

½ tsp. salt

1/3 cup sugar

1 TBSP baking powder

½ tsp. baking soda

¾ cup salted butter, softened

1 cup buttermilk

Preheat oven to 400°F. Combine dry ingredients then cut in butter until crumbly. Add buttermilk, stir to moisten—never beat biscuit dough. Turn dough out onto well-floured surface. Pat or roll out to ½-inch thickness and cut biscuits. Bake on an un-greased sheet or pan for approx. 13 mins. to desired brownness. Good hot or cold.

The Sweet Potato Queens' Field Guide to Men:
Every Man I Love is Either Married, Gay, or Dead
(Three Rivers Press, 2004), p. 217

BREAKFAST

AIG SOOFLE*

4 4-oz. cans diced green chilis

1 cup shredded Monterey Jack (or Pepper Jack) cheese

1 cup shredded Sharp Cheddar cheese

2 cups evaporated milk

4 eggs

1/3 cup flour

1 tsp. salt

Preheat oven to 350°F. In a greased, 2-qt. oblong, baking dish, layer peppers and cheeses. Use a blender or a food processor to combine remaining ingredients. Pour over peppers and cheese. Bake until knife comes out clean in center (about 45 mins.).

*Egg Soufflé, only not fancy.

This will one day appear in yet another *Sweet Potato Queens® book*, God willing.

BACON 'N EGGS, QUEEN-STYLE

18-20 eggs

2 lbs. Bryan® bacon
(1 to use; 1 to eat during construction)

6 TBSP salted butter

6 TBSP flour

2 cups milk

8 ozs. Cheese Whiz®

8 ozs. sour cream

Preheat oven to 350°F. Hard boil eggs and let 'em cool. Cook 2 lbs. Bryan® bacon and crumble up 1 lb. (Nibbling on the other during assembly of this dish.) Melt butter and add flour—stir it for about 30-60 seconds then slowly add milk and cook it until it gets thick—stirring constantly. Let it cool then add Cheese Whiz® (Regular or Hot) and sour cream. Peel the eggs then slice in half. Grease a 13" x 9" x 2" pan then put in a layer of the cheese sauce, a layer of egg slices, then a layer of bacon—repeating and ending with bacon, of course. Bake until bubbly. Eat with biscuits or toast, or even English muffins. Assemble ahead of time and keep refrigerated until ready to cook—**but do NOT freeze it!**

The Sweet Potato Queens' Big-Ass Cookbook (and Financial Planner)
(Three Rivers Press, 2003), p. 227

COUNTRY CLUB EGGS

1 dozen eggs, deviled

1 can tomato soup

Velveeta® cheese slices

Prepare 1 dozen deviled eggs. Preheat oven to 350°F. Put egg halves into an appropriate-sized baking dish and pour tomato soup over them. Top with slices of Velveeta® cheese. Bake until bubbly at edges.

God Save the Sweet Potato Queens
(Three Rivers Press, 2001), p. 221

and

The Sweet Potato Queens' Big-Ass Cookbook (and Financial Planner)
(Three Rivers Press, 2003), p. 261

EGG STUFF THAT GOES IN TORTILLAS

½ lb. Bryan® pork sausage, mild or hot

2 large potatoes, peeled and grated OR
1 bag fresh (not-frozen) hash browns

1 medium green pepper, chopped

½ cup onion, chopped

2 TBSP salted butter, melted

2 cups Pepper Jack cheese, shredded

1 4-ounce can chopped, green chilis

8 eggs

Taco sauce, hot or mild

Flour tortillas

Salt & pepper

Brown sausage then break into crumbles. Drain and set aside. In the same skillet, cook potatoes, pepper, and onions—cook until onions and peppers are soft. Potatoes may or may not brown. Stir in melted butter, cheese, chilis, and sausage. Salt and pepper to taste. (This mixture will freeze—can be thawed and added to eggs later.) To serve now, scramble the eggs and add to the mixture. Cook until eggs are desired doneness. Put desired amount on a tortilla, top with taco sauce. Roll and eat.

The Sweet Potato Queens' Big-Ass Cookbook (and Financial Planner)
(Three Rivers Press, 2003), p. 145

GRINNING, GRITS, AND GRILLADES
(AKA Grits & Grillades)

6-8 TBSP bacon drippings

2 lbs. thin meat (veal, round steak, pork),
pounded flat and cut into bite-size pieces

2 cups chopped onions

1 cup chopped green bell pepper

2 cloves garlic, minced

1 cup chopped tomatoes

½ tsp. thyme

4 TBSP flour

3 cups water

2 TBSP chopped parsley

2 tsp. salt

Tabasco®

Heat 4-6 TBSP bacon grease in large pot then brown the meat. (Do NOT crowd the pot.) Remove meat, lower heat and add onions, peppers, garlic, tomatoes, and thyme. Cook until tender. Remove from pan. Add remaining bacon grease to pan, heat and stir in flour—cook, stirring constantly, to make dark brown roux. Gradually add 1½ cups water, stirring until smooth, then add the cooked meat and vegetables, along with the parsley, salt, and Tabasco® to taste. Cook on *LOW* for 30 mins., then add remaining water and cook for another 45 mins. Serve over grits.

(ONLY use Regular or Quick grits. **_NEVER_** use Instant.)

(Continues on the next page.)

Grits

Regular or Quick grits—*never* Instant. Cook according to package directions. When grits are thickening, add butter and milk or cream—enough of each to cause grits to become thin again—and continue cooking over *LOW* heat, stirring constantly until thick. Salt and pepper to taste.

The Sweet Potato Queens' Big-Ass Cookbook (and Financial Planner)
(Three Rivers Press, 2003), p. 143

GRITS & GRILLADES
(AKA Grinning, Grits, and Grillades)

6-8 TBSP bacon drippings

2 lbs. thin meat (veal, round steak, pork),
pounded flat and cut into bite-size pieces

2 cups chopped onions

1 cup chopped green bell pepper

2 cloves garlic, minced

1 cup chopped tomatoes

½ tsp. thyme

4 TBSP flour

3 cups water

2 TBSP chopped parsley

2 tsp. salt

Tabasco®

Heat 4-6 TBSP bacon grease in large pot then brown the meat. (Do NOT crowd the pot.) Remove meat, lower heat and add onions, peppers, garlic, tomatoes, and thyme. Cook until tender. Remove from pan. Add remaining bacon grease to pan, heat and stir in flour—cook, stirring constantly, to make dark brown roux. Gradually add 1½ cups water, stirring until smooth, then add the cooked meat and vegetables, along with the parsley, salt, and Tabasco® to taste. Cook on *LOW* for 30 mins., then add remaining water and cook for another 45 mins. Serve over grits.

(ONLY use Regular or Quick grits. **_NEVER_** use Instant.)

(Continues on the next page.)

Grits

Regular or Quick grits—*never* Instant. Cook according to package directions. When grits are thickening, add butter and milk or cream—enough of each to cause grits to become thin again—and continue cooking over *LOW* heat, stirring constantly until thick. Salt and pepper to taste.

The Sweet Potato Queens' Big-Ass Cookbook (and Financial Planner)
(Three Rivers Press, 2003), p. 143

LITTLE JEFFREY'S FAVORITE MUFFINS

2 cups softened or melted salted butter

4 cups sugar

4 eggs, beaten

4 cups unsweetened applesauce

6 tsp. cinnamon

4 tsp. allspice

2 tsp. cloves

2 tsp. salt

4 tsp. baking soda

8 cups All-purpose flour

2 cups chopped pecans (optional)

Preheat oven to 350°F. In a large bowl, mix butter, and sugar, add eggs. Add applesauce and spices. Stir in flour, soda, salt, and pecans if using. Mix well. Spoon mixture into a greased, Texas-sized muffin pan or greased mini-muffin pans. Bake approx. 10 mins. for mini-muffins. Adjust times for larger muffins. Makes nearly endless supply of minis. Batter will keep for weeks in refrigerator, nearly forever in freezer.

Baked muffins also freeze well—reheat before serving. May half the recipe if you don't like having something so delicious so handy by. Still makes a lot though.

This will one day appear in yet another *Sweet Potato Queens® book*, God willing.

MICHAEL'S MAGICAL SWEET POTATO MUFFINS

1 cup dark brown sugar

½ cup canola oil

1 running over tsp. vanilla

2 eggs

2 cups flour

2 tsp. baking powder

1 tsp. cinnamon

1 tsp. nutmeg

½ tsp. allspice

½ tsp. salt

2 large sweet potatoes, baked or boiled,
peeled & mashed (may use canned)

½ cup raisins (optional)

1 cup pecan pieces (optional)

Preheat oven to 350°F. In a bowl, whisk together sugar, oil, vanilla, and eggs. In another bowl, combine dry ingredients. Add sweet potatoes to dry ingredients then stir in sugar mixture. (If desired, add ½ cup raisins and/or 1 cup pecan pieces.) Stir only until fully mixed. Bake in a greased muffin pan for 25-30 mins.

American Thighs:
The Sweet Potato Queens' Guide to Preserving Your Assets
(Simon & Schuster, 2009), p. 298

Pig Candy™

Bacon

Dark brown sugar

Chopped pecans

Preheat oven to 350°F. Line a rimmed cookie sheet with foil. Put a cooling rack on the foil-covered cookie sheet. NOTE: In the Recommendations section below is a great extra-large sheet and cooling rack. (Bigger is better and more is more, particularly when it comes to bacon!) Coat each slice of bacon with as much brown sugar as possible, put slices on the rack then sprinkle liberally with pecans, adding more brown sugar, if desired. Bake for at least 20 mins. or until desired doneness.

The Sweet Potato Queens' Big-Ass Cookbook (and Financial Planner)
(Three Rivers Press, 2003), p. 120

SHUT-UP, PIPPA, TOMATO GRAVY

Sausage patties

All-purpose flour

1 cup milk

1 small can Ro-tel® tomatoes, drained

Cook sausage in iron skillet, remove and put on paper towels. Drain most of the grease from the pan. Sprinkle a handful of All-purpose flour over the remaining grease then stir constantly until well-blended and golden brown. Add milk and cook, stirring, until smooth and thickened. Add drained tomatoes then cook, stirring, until desired consistency. Crumble sausage then add to gravy. Serve over hot biscuits.

The Sweet Potato Queens' Big-Ass Cookbook (and Financial Planner)
(Three Rivers Press, 2003), p. 230

SPUD STUD SCOTT'S SAUSAGE BALLS*
(AND CHEESE GRITS)

1 lb. regular breakfast sausage

1 lb. hot breakfast sausage

2 cups Sharp Cheddar cheese, shredded

2 cups Pepper Jack cheese, shredded

1 TBSP Worcestershire sauce

4 cups Original Bisquick™ Pancake & Baking Mix

Preheat oven to 350°F. Combine all ingredients and mix thoroughly. Form into bite-sized balls (a melon baller works great). Bake on a greased cookie sheet for 15 mins. if to be served immediately.

For FREEZING: Bake for 13 minutes so they are formed and will not stick together in the freezer bag. They will not dry out when reheated.

To REHEAT: Put frozen sausage balls onto a greased cookie sheet and bake at 350°F for 15 mins.

*Excellent served with Cheese Grits for breakfast or as a stand-alone appetizer.

(Continues on the next page.)

Cheese Grits

Regular or Quick grits
(*never* Instant)

Salted butter

Milk or cream

Sharp Cheddar cheese, shredded

Salt

Red pepper

Regular or Quick grits—*never* Instant. Cook according to package directions. When grits are thickening, add butter, and milk or cream—enough of each to cause the grits to become thin again—and continue cooking over *LOW* heat, stirring constantly until it begins to thicken again, then dump in copious amounts of shredded Sharp Cheddar cheese. Stir constantly over *LOW* heat until cheese is melted and well blended. Salt and red pepper to taste.

This will one day appear in yet another *Sweet Potato Queens® book*, God willing.

CASEROLES

CRAZY-GOOD CABBAGE

1 small cabbage, cut up

1 medium Vidalia (or other sweet) onion, chopped

1 10.5-oz. can cream of chicken soup*

1 cup mayo

½ stick salted butter, melted

Topping

1 stick salted butter, melted

1 cup Sharp Cheddar cheese, shredded

1 sleeve Ritz® crackers, crushed

Preheat oven to 350°F. Grease a 13″ x 9″ x 2″ baking dish. Put chopped cabbage in dish, top with chopped onions. In a bowl, mix together soup, mayo, and butter. Pour over vegetables.

In a bowl, mix together butter, cheese, and cracker crumbs. Spread over top of everything in the baking dish. Bake approx. 45 mins.

*If you prefer not to use canned soup, you may substitute a scratch-made…

(Continues on next page.)

Béchamel Sauce

½ cup chicken broth

½ cup milk

3 TBSP butter

3 TBSP flour

Salt and pepper to taste

Melt butter and flour together in a small sauce pan, stirring constantly. Slowly add in broth and milk while bringing to a *Gentle Boil* and cooking until desired thickness is reached.

This will one day appear in yet another *Sweet Potato Queens® book*, God willing.

(THE) CUTEST BOY IN THE WORLD'S ("TCBITW'S") MAMA'S BROCCOLI CASSEROLE

2 10-oz. pkgs. frozen broccoli florets, cooked and drained

½ stick salted butter

1 chopped onion

1 can cream of mushroom soup

1 roll Kraft® garlic cheese*

1 can sliced water chestnuts, drained

4-oz. can sliced mushrooms, drained

½ cup sliced almonds, toasted

Cornflake crumbs

Preheat oven to 350°F. Sauté onion in butter. Combine broccoli and onions, stir in soup, cheese, water chestnuts, mushrooms, and almonds. Top with cornflake crumbs. Bake until bubbly. Can double and can freeze.

*Kraft® quit making these; so, here is a recipe equaling 2 rolls.

Mix together all of these ingredients:

¾ lb. each Cheddar and American cheese, shredded

¼ lb. Velveeta®

2 ozs. cream cheese

½ tsp. seasoned salt

Garlic powder to taste

The Sweet Potato Queens' Field Guide to Men:
Every Man I Love is Either Married, Gay, or Dead
(Three Rivers Press, 2004), p. 216

GORILLA CASSEROLE

1½ lbs. cooked pasta shells or penne

2 TBSP olive oil

2½ lbs. ground chuck

2 cups chopped onions

3 ribs chopped celery (with leaves)

3 large carrots, grated

2 2-lb. cans Italian-style tomatoes

1½ tsp. oregano

1 tsp. black pepper

1 tsp. garlic powder

1 10-oz. pkg. frozen chopped spinach, thawed and drained

Parmesan cheese

Salt

Preheat oven to 350°F. Brown beef in oil, then add onion, celery, and carrots. Cook until tender, then add tomatoes and seasonings. Simmer for an hour. Add pasta and spinach to mixture. Salt to taste. Put into two (2) greased 13″ x 9″ x 2″ pans, top with liberal amount of Parmesan then bake until bubbly.

The Sweet Potato Queens' Big-Ass Cookbook (and Financial Planner)
(Three Rivers Press, 2003), p. 210

GREAT GOUDA GOODNESS

2 TBSP salted butter

1 large Vidalia onion, sliced into thin rounds

Garlic to taste

1/8 cup water

1 cup heavy cream

½ cup cottage cheese

1 tsp. salt

1 cup Parmesan

2 large zucchini, sliced into ¼ inch rounds

2 large yellow squash, sliced ¼ inch rounds

½ cup crisp bacon (optional)

1½ cups smoked Gouda, shredded

Preheat oven to 400°F. Melt butter in an iron skillet or stainless steel skillet with an oven-safe handle. Add onion then cook until translucent. Add garlic and cook 2-3 mins. Add squash and water. Stir then cover. Cook just until squash softens. Uncover and cook until water is gone. (If too much liquid, slide squash to one side of pan, wad up paper towels and just sop it up.) Mix cream and cottage cheese together then stir into squash. Cook, stirring, until it begins to thicken slightly. Stir in Parmesan and salt. Remove from heat then top with bacon (if using) and spread Gouda over the top. Bake for 20 mins. or until cheese is brown. Let stand several mins. before serving.

This will one day appear in yet another *Sweet Potato Queens® book*, God willing.

HIGH OCTANE MAC 'N' CHEESE

1 lb. penne pasta, cooked *al dente*

1½ lbs. ground chuck

2-3 TBSP olive oil

1 cup chopped onions

1 cup chopped bell pepper

1 tsp. salt

2 TBSP chili powder

1 14.5-oz. can diced tomatoes with jalapeños (plain, if preferred)

1 15-oz. can tomato sauce

1 7-oz. can chopped chilis

1 cup water

2 cups cheese (Cheddar or Pepper Jack)

In a deep skillet, brown beef and reserve. In the same skillet, cook onions and peppers in olive oil until tender. Add salt, chili powder, tomatoes, tomato sauce, and chilis. Simmer for a few minutes. Add back the browned beef, chopping into bite-size chunks. Add water and *Simmer* on *LOW* for 5-10 mins. Remove from heat then stir in pasta and cheese. Mix well then serve.

Fat Is The New 30:
The Sweet Potato Queens' Guide to Coping with (the crappy parts of) Life
(Amazon Publishing, 2012), p. 137

LATIN LASAGNA
(AKA Spud Stud Scott's Lasagna Latino)

¼ cup butter

1 med. onion, chopped

1/3 cup All-purpose Flour

1 TBSP cumin

1¾ cups chicken broth

1 cup milk

4 - 4½ cups shredded Pepper Jack cheese, divided

1 lb. raw Mexican chorizo, casings removed

1 lb. ground turkey

2 TBSP Worcestershire

1 TBSP lemon juice

1 TBSP oregano

Paprika to taste

Salt and pepper to taste

6 to 8 ripe, black-skinned plantains, peeled, halved horizontally and
thinly sliced lengthwise

Paprika to taste

Preheat oven to 350°F. Melt butter in a sauce pan over *MEDIUM* heat; add onion, cook until translucent, add salt and pepper to taste. Add cumin and mix in flour; stirring, cook for 1 min. Slowly add broth, stirring to avoid lumps; then, add milk, stirring constantly until it begins to thicken—about 8-10 mins.

(Continues on the next page.)

Add 2 cups of the Pepper Jack, cooking and stirring until all melted. Remove from heat, pour into bowl, put sheet of plastic wrap directly on surface of sauce to avoid a skin forming.

Heat large deep iron skillet or large stainless frying pan over *MEDIUM-HIGH* heat and cook chorizo until it begins browning, about 4 mins., breaking up pieces with wooden spoon while it cooks. Add turkey and continue to cook until both meats are browned, about 8-10 mins. Drain excess fat from skillet/pan. Stir in Worcestershire, lemon juice, and oregano.

Line bottom of a greased 13" x 9" x 2" baking dish with 1 layer of plantains (about 1/3 of slices)—don't overlap them. Top plantains with half the meat mixture, covering plantains evenly. Top with half the cheese sauce, spreading evenly with spatula. Add another layer of plantain slices, cover with remaining meat mixture and sauce. Add final layer of plantains, cover with remaining Pepper Jack, sprinkle with paprika. Bake until bubbly, about 45 mins. Let cool for 10 minutes before cutting to serve.

*Unbaked casserole freezes well.

This will one day appear in yet another *Sweet Potato Queens® book*, God willing.

LITTLE LARVA'S HOMICIDAL MANIAC AND CHEESE

2 lbs. cooked macaroni

8-10 slices cooked bacon

½ stick salted butter

2 cups Gruyere cheese

1½ cups milk

1 can Cheddar cheese soup

3 cups Extra-Sharp Cheddar cheese, shredded

1 tsp. dry mustard

1 cup sour cream

In a small sauce pan, melt butter and Gruyere cheese in milk. Put macaroni in Crock-Pot® and add cheese soup, Cheddar, mustard, and sour cream, stir. Add milk mixture and crumbled bacon then stir again. Cook on *LOW* for about 3 hours.

American Thighs:
The Sweet Potato Queens' Guide to Preserving Your Assets
(Simon & Schuster, 2009), p. 292

LOVE-APPLE (TOMATO) PIE
(regular or crustless)

5 medium tomatoes, skinned, chopped into chunks

1 medium onion, chopped

½ clove garlic

1 TBSP dark brown sugar

2 TBSP chopped basil (fresh or freeze-dried)

Salt to taste

1 cup shredded Swiss cheese

1 cup shredded Sharp Cheddar cheese

¾ cup mayo

1 baked 10" pie shell (cooled) — OPTIONAL

Preheat oven to 400°F. Peel and chop tomatoes. Mix all ingredients and bake in a greased 13" x 9" x 2" pan for 20-25 mins.; or, spoon into pie crust and bake. Let stand for several minutes after baking.

This will one day appear in yet another *Sweet Potato Queens® book*, God willing.

MAKETH ME TO LIE DOWN IN MAC 'N' CHEESE

1 12-oz. pkg. pasta shells or Rotini

¼ cup salted butter

¼ cup flour

2 cups hot milk

1 tsp. seasoned salt

½ tsp. black pepper

1 heaping cup, shredded Cheddar cheese

12 strips bacon, fried, crumbled

1 cup chopped onions

1 cup sliced fresh mushrooms

2 cups shredded Monterey Jack cheese

Tater Tots

Parmesan cheese

Preheat oven to 375°F. Cook then drain pasta. In a small sauce pan, melt butter and stir in flour. Add milk, salt, and pepper. Cook, stirring, until it begins to thicken—add Cheddar; cook, stirring, until it's melted and smooth. Cook onions and mushrooms in grease from the bacon. In a greased 13" x 9" x 2" pan, combine pasta, onions, mushrooms, sauce, and bacon. Stir in Monterey Jack cheese. Cover

(Continues on the next page.)

top with Tater Tots and sprinkle liberally with Parmesan. Bake for an hour or until bubbly and Tots are crispy; or, bake for 40 mins. and then *Broil* to brown Tots.

The Sweet Potato Queens' First Big-Ass Novel:
Stuff We Didn't Actually Do, but Could Have, and May Yet.
(Simon & Schuster, 2008), p. 285

MANLY, MEATLY SQUASH

3 large Summer squash (Yellow or Zucchini)

½ cup white rice, uncooked

2 cups water

1 tsp. salt

½ tsp. black pepper

1 TBSP bacon drippings

2 cups stewed tomatoes

1 tsp. garlic, chopped

½ lb. ground chuck

Preheat oven to 350°F. Cut squash in half, lengthwise, remove seeds. Put water and salt in covered pot, bring to *Boil*. Put squash, cut side down, in water then cook over *MEDIUM* heat, 5 mins. until tender. Remove and drain. Heat drippings in skillet, add garlic and beef—cook until brown. Add rice, salt, pepper, and tomatoes. Cover then cook over *LOW* heat until liquid is absorbed. Spoon mixture into squash shells, top with half the sauce and bake for 15-20 mins. Pour remaining sauce over squash before serving.

(Continues on the next page.)

Sauce

2 TBSP salted butter

2 TBSP flour

½ tsp. dry mustard

¼ tsp. salt

¼ tsp. red pepper

1 cup milk

¼ to ½ cup Sharp Cheddar cheese

Melt butter in sauce pan, add flour and stir until blended. Add other ingredients and cook, stirring, over *MEDIUM* heat until thickened. Add the cheese and cook, stirring, until melted.

The Sweet Potato Queens' Field Guide to Men:
Every Man I Love is Either Married, Gay, or Dead
(Three Rivers Press, 2004), p. 214

MISS LEXIE'S PINEAPPLE CASSEROLE
(AKA Pineapple Stuff)

1 20-oz. can pineapple in juice, chunks or tidbits

3 TBSP juice

½ cup sugar

3 TBSP flour

1 cup Sharp Cheddar cheese, shredded

2 TBSP salted butter

½ cup Ritz® cracker crumbs

Preheat oven to 350°F. Drain pineapple and retain 3 TBSP juice. In a bowl, mix juice with sugar and flour. Stir mixture into pineapple with cheese. Put into a greased, appropriate-sized baking dish. In a sauce pan, melt butter then stir in cracker crumbs. Top pineapple with buttered crumbs then bake for 20-30 mins. Can be frozen.

The Sweet Potato Queens Book of Love
(Three Rivers Press, 1999), p. 182

and

The Sweet Potato Queens' Big-Ass Cookbook (and Financial Planner)
(Three Rivers Press, 2003), p. 258

PINEAPPLE STUFF
(AKA Miss Lexie's Pineapple Casserole)

1 20-oz. can pineapple in juice, chunks or tidbits

3 TBSP juice

½ cup sugar

3 TBSP flour

1 cup Sharp Cheddar cheese, shredded

2 TBSP salted butter

½ cup Ritz® cracker crumbs

Preheat oven to 350°F. Drain pineapple and retain 3 TBSP juice. In a bowl, mix juice with sugar and flour. Stir mixture into pineapple with cheese. Put into a greased, appropriate-sized baking dish. In a sauce pan, melt butter then stir in cracker crumbs. Top pineapple with buttered crumbs then bake for 20-30 mins. Can be frozen.

The Sweet Potato Queens Book of Love
(Three Rivers Press, 1999), p. 182

and

The Sweet Potato Queens' Big-Ass Cookbook (and Financial Planner)
(Three Rivers Press, 2003), p. 258

SPINACH MADELINE

2 bags (20 – 24 ozs.) frozen chopped or cut leaf spinach

4 TBSP salted butter

2 TBSP flour

2 TBSP onion, chopped

Velveeta® Jalapeño cheese (*Important note below), cut into small chunks

½ cup evaporated milk

½ cup "vegetable liquor"

¾ tsp. celery salt

¾ tsp. garlic salt

Cayenne pepper to taste

1 TBSP Worcestershire sauce

1 sleeve Ritz® crackers, crushed (optional)

3 TBSP salted butter, melted (optional)

Cook spinach in sauce pan with 2 cups water. Drain but reserve ½ cup of the liquid ("vegetable liquor"). In another medium sauce pan, melt butter over *LOW* heat, add flour, stirring until blended and smooth. Slowly add reserved "vegetable liquor", stirring constantly. Add evaporated milk and cook, stirring, until it begins to thicken. Add seasonings and Velveeta®; continue cooking, stirring until all is melted. Stir in spinach. May serve immediately.

(Continues on the next page.)

For best flavor: put into a greased 1½ qt. casserole dish, let cool, cover, then refrigerate overnight. Top with buttered Ritz® crumbs (combine crushed crackers with 3 TBSP melted butter) and bake at 350°F, until bubbly.

* Velveeta® Jalapeño is not available everywhere. May use plain Velveeta® and add 2-3 TBSP diced jalapeño or to taste.

HIGHLY recommend doubling this recipe.

This will one day appear in yet another *Sweet Potato Queens® book*, God willing.

SPUD STUD SCOTT'S CHICKEN TAMALE CASSEROLE

1 8.5 oz. box Jiffy® Cornbread mix

1 14.5 oz. can cream corn

1 14.5 oz. can whole kernel corn

1 14.5 oz. can diced tomatoes with jalapeños

2 eggs, beaten

½ cup milk

1 tsp. chili powder

½ tsp. cumin

2 cups taco cheese blend, shredded, divided (more if desired)

2 10-oz. cans red enchilada sauce

3 cups cooked chicken thighs, cut bite-size

Preheat oven to 400°F. Grease 13" x 9" x 2" baking dish. Mix together Jiffy®, corn, eggs, milk, spices, and 1 cup of cheese. Stir well and pour into baking dish. Bake for 30 mins. until lightly browned. Remove from oven and pierce baked cornbread all over with tip of wooden spoon handle then pour the enchilada sauce over it. Top with chopped chicken and remaining cheese. Bake for additional 20 mins. Cool for 10 mins. before serving.

This will one day appear in yet another *Sweet Potato Queens®* book, God willing.

Spud Stud Scott's Great Nasty Recipe

1 lb. ground beef

2 TBSP minced onion

1 can cream of chicken soup

1 can Cheddar cheese soup

2 cups Velveeta®, shredded

2 dozen Tater Tots

Preheat oven to 350°F. In a skillet, brown beef then drain. Add onions to skillet and cook until tender. In a greased, appropriate-sized baking dish, combine half the meat with cream of chicken soup. Add remaining meat and top with cheese soup. Add Velveeta®, then on top of that, put the Tater Tots. Bake for about an hour.

American Thighs:
The Sweet Potato Queens' Guide to Preserving Your Assets
(Simon & Schuster, 2009), p. 290

Spud Stud Scott's Lasagna Latino
(AKA Latin Lasagna)

¼ cup butter

1 med. onion, chopped

1/3 cup All-purpose Flour

1 TBSP cumin

1¾ cups chicken broth

1 cup milk

4 - 4½ cups shredded Pepper Jack cheese, divided

1 lb. raw Mexican chorizo, casings removed

1 lb. ground turkey

2 TBSP Worcestershire

1 TBSP lemon juice

1 TBSP oregano

Paprika to taste

Salt and pepper to taste

6 to 8 ripe, black-skinned plantains, peeled, halved horizontally and thinly sliced lengthwise

Paprika to taste

Preheat oven to 350°F. Melt butter in a sauce pan over *MEDIUM* heat; add onion, cook until translucent, add salt and pepper to taste. Add cumin and mix in flour; stirring, cook for 1 min. Slowly add broth, stirring to avoid lumps; then, add milk, stirring constantly until it begins to thicken—about 8-10 mins.

(Continues on the next page.)

Add 2 cups of the Pepper Jack, cooking and stirring until all melted. Remove from heat, pour into bowl, put sheet of plastic wrap directly on surface of sauce to avoid a skin forming.

Heat large deep iron skillet or large stainless frying pan over *MEDIUM-HIGH* heat and cook chorizo until it begins browning, about 4 mins., breaking up pieces with wooden spoon while it cooks. Add turkey and continue to cook until both meats are browned, about 8-10 mins. Drain excess fat from skillet/pan. Stir in Worcestershire, lemon juice, and oregano.

Line bottom of a greased 13" x 9" x 2" baking dish with 1 layer of plantains (about 1/3 of slices)—don't overlap them. Top plantains with half the meat mixture, covering plantains evenly. Top with half the cheese sauce, spreading evenly with spatula. Add another layer of plantain slices, cover with remaining meat mixture and sauce. Add final layer of plantains, cover with remaining Pepper Jack, sprinkle with paprika. Bake until bubbly, about 45 mins. Let cool for 10 minutes before cutting to serve.

*Unbaked casserole freezes well.

This will one day appear in yet another *Sweet Potato Queens®* *book*, God willing.

TCBITW's Favorite Big Giant Casserole*

3 lbs. ground chuck

1 cup chopped onions

2 12-oz. bags frozen chopped or cut spinach,

thaw and squeeze out water

2 8-oz. blocks cream cheese, softened

2 14.5-oz. cans diced tomatoes with jalapeños

4 TBSP chili powder

2 cups shredded Cheddar or Pepper Jack cheese

Salt to taste

Preheat oven to 350°F. In a deep iron skillet, large stainless frying pan, or microwave steaming container, brown and drain beef. Put onions in microwave-safe bowl with frozen spinach and cook for 5-7 mins. Pour off any excess liquid. Combine all ingredients, except cheese, and mix well. Put into a greased, appropriate-sized baking dish. Top with liberal amount of cheese. Bake for 25-30 mins. until bubbling around edges and cheese browned as desired. Freezes well.

*The Cutest Boy in the World, my own personal husband, Kyle Jennings, would eat this every day…if I let him.

Makes enough for 2 big pans — freeze one.

Leftovers (if there are any) are excellent additions to scrambled eggs.

This will one day appear in yet another *Sweet Potato Queens®* book, God willing.

CHICKEN

BETTER'N HIS OWN MAMA'S CHICKEN AND DUMPLINS

1 large onion, chopped

3 carrots, sliced thin

4 stalks celery, chopped

4 TBSP oil

3 cups cooked chicken, bite-size pieces

6½ cups chicken broth

1½ cups self-rising flour

¼ cup shortening

2 TBSP chopped fresh parsley

In a large pot, cook onions, carrots, and celery in the oil until tender. Add chicken and broth then *Simmer* over lowered heat for 15-20 mins.

To make dumplings: Cut shortening into flour until crumb texture forms. Add parsley and ½ cup broth then stir just until moistened. Drop dough by tablespoon into simmering chicken mixture, cover pot and LEAVE COVERED while cooking for 15 mins.

The Sweet Potato Queens' Field Guide to Men:
Every Man I Love is Either Married, Gay, or Dead
(Three Rivers Press, 2004), p. 226

BRIGHT-SIDE-OF-THE-ROAD CHICKEN

8 to 10 chicken thighs or breasts*

8 oz. cream cheese, softened

½ stick salted butter, softened

¼ cup heavy cream

¼ cup chopped onions

½ tsp. seasoned salt

Shredded Sharp Cheddar or Pepper Jack cheese

Preheat oven to 375°F. Put chicken pieces into a greased baking pan. Combine cream cheese, butter, cream, onions, and seasoned salt. Spread over chicken. Top with cheese. Bake for 35-40 mins. or until done.

*Personal preference is bone-in, skin-on chicken but boneless, skinless will work.

This will one day appear in yet another *Sweet Potato Queens® book*, God willing.

CHICKEN HOWDY

2 cups "pork panko"* or bread crumbs

¾ cup Parmesan

1 tsp. paprika

1 tsp. garlic salt

4 TBSP fresh parsley or
4 tsp. dried parsley

1 stick salted butter, melted

1 tsp. Worcestershire sauce

1 tsp. dry mustard

8 chicken thighs or

8 breast halves, boneless skinless**

Preheat oven to 350°F. Line a 13" x 9" x 2" pan with foil. Mix together crumbs, Parmesan, paprika, garlic salt, and parsley. Melt butter, add Worcestershire and mustard. Dip chicken in butter mix and then in the crumb mix. Put into pan and pour remaining butter mix over top. Bake 45 mins.

*Pork panko—crushed pork skins, plain or barbecue.

**For main dish, cook whole chicken pieces. As appetizers, cut into strips.

This will one day appear in yet another *Sweet Potato Queens®* *book*, God willing.

CHICKEN SHIT

3 cups cooked chicken, cubed

1 can cream of chicken soup

6 oz. sour cream

½ tsp. black pepper

¼ cup milk

Ritz® cracker crumbs

Salted butter

Preheat oven to 350°F. Combine chicken, soup, sour cream, pepper, and milk into a greased, appropriate- sized baking dish. Top with cracker crumbs and butter pats. Bake for 30 mins. Serve with rice.

The Sweet Potato Queens' First Big-Ass Novel:
Stuff We Didn't Actually Do, but Could Have, and May Yet.
(Simon & Schuster, 2008), p. 283

DEATH CHICKEN

6+ slices bacon (uncooked)

1 cup rice (uncooked)

Chicken pieces (with skin is best)

Paprika

1 can cream of chicken soup

1 cup water

1 tsp. oregano

2-3 TBSP dried parsley flakes

Pinch garlic salt and nutmeg

Salt to taste

Pepper to taste

Rice

Preheat oven to 300°F. Line 13" x 9" x 2" pan with bacon (6 or more slices). Pour uncooked rice over bacon, top with chicken pieces then lightly season with salt, pepper, and paprika. Whisk together soup, water, and seasonings—pour over chicken then cover tightly with *HEAVY* aluminum foil. Cook for 2 hours *without uncovering.*

God Save the Sweet Potato Queens
(Three Rivers Press, 2001), p. 212

and

The Sweet Potato Queens' Big-Ass Cookbook (and Financial Planner)
(Three Rivers Press, 2003), p. 259

HIGH-KICKIN' CHICKEN

4 TBSP salted butter

3 TBSP olive oil

8 or 10 pieces of chicken* (thighs or breasts)

½ cup raspberry vinegar

1 cup chicken broth

1 cup heavy cream

Salt to taste

Melt butter in skillet with olive oil over *MEDIUM* heat then brown chicken on both sides. Remove chicken and add vinegar to pan, stirring to remove any bits stuck to bottom. Add broth and stir well then put chicken back in, cover pan and *Simmer* for 20 mins. or until done through. Remove chicken and keep warm. Continue cooking the broth mixture in skillet to reduce and thicken slightly. Add the cream in slowly and continue cooking over *MEDIUM* heat until thickened. Pour sauce over chicken and serve.

*Personal preference is bone-in, skin-on; but, boneless, skinless may be used.

This will one day appear in yet another *Sweet Potato Queens®* *book*, God willing.

SPUD STUD SCOTT'S MAMA'S CHICKEN

4 large chicken breasts or 8 thighs,
boneless, skinless, cut into 2 inch pieces

1 stick salted butter

1½ sleeves Saltine crackers, crushed

2 cans condensed cream of chicken soup

16 ozs. sour cream

1 TBSP dried tarragon (more or less to suit preference)

Preheat oven to 350°F. Put butter into 13" x 9" x 2" pan then put into oven to melt during preheating. Mix soup, sour cream, and tarragon then set aside. When butter is melted, tilt and rotate pan to coat the bottom and sides of pan. Sprinkle cracker crumbs over the butter and completely cover the bottom of the pan evenly. Put the chicken in the pan. Spread the soup mixture evenly over the chicken and bake for 35-40 mins. Let stand for a few mins. before serving.

*Scott's Mama always served this with tiny LeSeur® green peas cooked in butter; so, we recommend that to you as well.

This will one day appear in yet another *Sweet Potato Queens® book*, God willing.

DIPS & APPETIZERS

ALPHA MOM STUFF IN A PUMPKIN

4 TBSP salted butter, melted

½ tsp. ground ginger

Salad oil

2 lbs. ground pork sausage

1 lb. ground round

½ cup chopped celery

1 cup chopped onion

4 cups croutons

1 cup dark brown sugar

1 cup chopped walnuts

2 TBSP orange juice

1 large bag Fritos® Scoops

Preheat oven to 375°F. Wash pumpkin, then cut off the top and hollow it out. Brush inside with 2 TBSP melted butter and ground ginger. Brush the outside of it with oil. Put the top on and bake the whole pumpkin for 30 mins. In a skillet, brown ground pork sausage with ground round and drain well. Add chopped celery and

(Continues on the next page.)

chopped onion and cook until onion is translucent—then add croutons, chopped walnuts, and dark brown sugar. Stir in melted butter and orange juice. Put it all in the pumpkin and bake it for 30 mins. Serve with Fritos®.

The Sweet Potato Queens' Guide to Raising Children for Fun and Profit
(Simon & Schuster, 2008), p. 78

ARMADILLO DIP

1 lb. ground chuck

1 or 2 pkgs. taco seasoning

Hot sauce

Mexican Velveeta® (hot or mild)

1 large bag Fritos® or Tostitos®

In a skillet, brown ground chuck and drain. Add taco seasoning (to taste), hot sauce (to taste), and Velveeta®. Stir over *LOW* heat until melted. Serve with Fritos® or Tostitos®.

The Sweet Potato Queens Book of Love
(Three Rivers Press, 1999), p. 172

and

The Sweet Potato Queens' Big-Ass Cookbook (and Financial Planner)
(Three Rivers Press, 2003), p. 255

ARMADILLO TAILS

Fresh jalapeños

Grilled chicken breasts, cut up
(May use pre-packaged)

1 8-oz. pkg. cream cheese

1 or 2 TBSP chili powder (to taste)

Bacon (uncooked)

PUT ON FOOD PREP GLOVES. Gloved-up, cut peppers in half, lengthwise, remove seeds and ribs. Microwave cream cheese on *LOW* in a bowl until it gets soft then stir in chili powder. Over-stuff each jalapeño half with cream cheese mixture then top with chicken. Wrap the whole thing in BACON. Secure with toothpick. Grill both sides in a closed grill basket until the bacon is cooked to desired doneness.

CAUTION:
Do not eat until cool!

The Sweet Potato Queens' Field Guide to Men:
Every Man I Love is Either Married, Gay, or Dead
(Three Rivers Press, 2004), p. 221

ARTICHOKE NIBBLES

2 6-oz. jars artichoke hearts

1 small onion

1 clove garlic

4 eggs

¼ cup bread crumbs

¼ tsp. salt

¼ tsp. black or red pepper

1/8 tsp. oregano

1/8 tsp. chili powder

2 cups Sharp Cheddar, shredded

2 TBSP chopped parsley

Preheat oven to 325°F. Drain the juice from one 6-ounce jar of artichoke hearts into a frying pan—drain a second 6-ounce jar of artichoke hearts down the drain. Chop all the artichokes and set aside. Chop onion and garlic clove and sauté in the artichoke juice for about 5 mins. In a mixing bowl, beat eggs then add in bread crumbs, salt, black or red pepper, oregano, and chili powder. Stir in Sharp Cheddar, chopped parsley, and the chopped artichokes. Bake it in a large baking pan for about 30 mins. Cut it into squares when it's cool.

The Sweet Potato Queens' Wedding Planner and Divorce Guide
(Crown Publishers, 2007), *Divorce Guide* side, p. 113

Bacon and Beagle Dicks

1 lb. thin-sliced, hickory smoked bacon, cut into thirds
1 16-oz. pkg. Li'l Smokies® cocktail sausages
Dark brown sugar

Preheat oven to 350°F. Wrap each sausage with 1 piece bacon and secure with toothpick. Place on foil-lined cookie sheet about 1 inch apart and cover each with dark brown sugar. Bake until bacon is desired doneness. Excellent hot or room temp.

The Sweet Potato Queens' Field Guide to Men:
Every Man I Love is Either Married, Gay, or Dead
(Three Rivers Press, 2004), p. 219

BITCH BACON BREADSTICKS

3 lbs. thin-sliced bacon

3 3-oz. boxes Grissini breadsticks

1/3 cup dark brown sugar

3 TBSP chili powder

Preheat oven to 350°F. Let bacon sit at room temp for about 10 mins. Wrap 1 slice bacon around each bread stick. Mix well together dark brown sugar and chili powder in a long shallow dish (long enough in which to lay the breadsticks). Roll bacon-wrapped breadsticks in sugar mixture then place breadsticks on a broiler pan, about ½ inch apart. Bake for about 20 mins. (Sugar will caramelize in the bacon fat, turning bacon golden.) Remove rack, loosen breadsticks with spatula and cool to room temperature.

The Sweet Potato Queens' Big-Ass Cookbook (and Financial Planner)
(Three Rivers Press, 2003), p. 78

Bitch Bar™ Bacon Swimps

Thin-sliced bacon

Fresh shrimp, large

Pepper Jack cheese

Barbecue sauce
(Sweet, hot variety such as McClard's®)

Microwave bacon until NEARLY done. Peel, de-vein, and butterfly shrimp. Put a hunk of Pepper Jack cheese in the butterflied shrimp and wrap each in a piece of nearly-cooked bacon. Grill until shrimp turns pink and the bacon finishes cooking. Right before removing shrimp from grill, slather each with your favorite sweet, hot barbecue sauce. Allow to cool slightly before eating.

CAUTION:
Cheese is molten lava-like!

The Sweet Potato Queens' Big-Ass Cookbook (and Financial Planner)
(Three Rivers Press, 2003), p. 79

CAN'T DIE WITHOUT DEVILED EGGS

1 dozen eggs

2 TBSP sweet pickle relish

2-3 TBSP Hellman's® Real Mayonnaise

2 tsp. yellow mustard

Salt

Pepper

Hard boil eggs. When cool, peel them then cut in half and remove yolks. Mash yolks with other all other ingredients then spoon or pipe into egg white halves. Salt and pepper to taste.

The Sweet Potato Queens' First Big-Ass Novel:
Stuff We Didn't Actually Do, but Could Have, and May Yet.
(Simon & Schuster, 2008), p. 284.

CHICKEN HOWDY

2 cups "pork panko"* or bread crumbs

¾ cup Parmesan

1 tsp. paprika

1 tsp. garlic salt

4 TBSP fresh parsley or
4 tsp. dried parsley

1 stick salted butter, melted

1 tsp. Worcestershire sauce

1 tsp. dry mustard

8 chicken thighs or

8 breast halves, boneless skinless**

Preheat oven to 350°F. Line a 13" x 9" x 2" pan with foil. Mix together crumbs, Parmesan, paprika, garlic salt, and parsley. Melt butter, add Worcestershire and mustard. Dip chicken in butter mix and then in the crumb mix. Put into pan and pour remaining butter mix over top. Bake 45 mins.

*Pork panko—crushed pork skins, plain or barbecue.

**For main dish, cook whole chicken pieces. As appetizers, cut into strips.

This will one day appear in yet another *Sweet Potato Queens® book*, God willing.

HEAVEN ON A CRACKER

2 8-oz. pkgs. cream cheese

2/3 cup Miracle Whip® (NO substitutes!)

8 oz. Swiss cheese, shredded

1-3 TBSP green onion, minced

16 slices bacon, cooked, crumbled

1 sleeve Ritz® crackers, crushed

1 box Ritz® crackers or 1 large bag Fritos® or tortilla chips

Soften cream cheese in the microwave (remove foil wrapper first). Mix cream cheese, Miracle Whip®, Swiss cheese, and green onion. Put mixture in a microwave-safe dish. Stir up cooked, crumbled bacon with crushed Ritz® crackers. Put that mixture on top of the cheese mixture and microwave until hot all the way through (shouldn't take more than 2 to 3 mins.). Serve with tortilla chips, Ritz® crackers or Fritos®.

The Sweet Potato Queens' Big-Ass Cookbook (and Financial Planner)
(Three Rivers Press, 2003), p. 70

JODY'S BIG BITES

1 TBSP dill

1 TBSP caraway seed

1 TBSP crushed red pepper

1 pkg. dry Ranch dressing mix

1½ cups canola oil

4 sleeves Saltine crackers

Combine first 5 ingredients. Mix well and divide between two 1-gallon Ziploc-type bags and put 2 sleeves of Saltines in each bag. Let sit overnight, turning frequently to allow for even absorption. Next day—pour out any unabsorbed oil and put the crackers in a fresh Ziploc-type bag. They will stay crispy.

The Sweet Potato Queens' Wedding Planner and Divorce Guide
(Crown Publishers, 2007), *Wedding Planner* side, p. 81

OLIVE YUM YUMS

4 oz. cream cheese, softened

1 10-oz. jar Colossal green olives, with pimento

1 cup chopped pecans

Drain and blot dry olives. Form a ball of cream cheese around each olive and roll in chopped pecans. Refrigerate until the cream cheese has reset.

The Sweet Potato Queens' Wedding Planner and Divorce Guide
(Crown Publishers, 2007), *Wedding Planner* side, p. 82

ONE MORE REASON TO EAT FRITOS®

4 ripe avocados, peeled & seeded

16 oz. sour cream

3 oz. cream cheese

1 4-oz. can diced green chilis

1 10-oz. can Ro-tel® tomatoes

2 tsp. salt

1 TBSP garlic powder

1 tsp. lemon juice

1 large bag Fritos® Scoops

Combine all ingredients, except Fritos®, in bowl of food processor and *Pulse* until completely blended. Eat with Fritos® Scoops, of course.

The Sweet Potato Queens' Wedding Planner and Divorce Guide
(Crown Publishers, 2007), *Divorce Guide* side, p. 114

Queen Chris and Bob-Daddy's "Melted Salad"

1 10-oz. pkg. frozen chopped spinach, thawed and drained

2 8-oz. pkgs. cream cheese, softened

2 cups Monterey Jack cheese, shredded

1 cup Parmesan cheese, shredded

1 one small onion, minced

1 14-oz. can chopped artichoke hearts, drained

2 10-oz. cans Ro-tel® tomatoes

2 tsp. ground cumin

2 tsp. chili powder

1 tsp. garlic powder

1 large bag Fritos® Scoops

Preheat oven to 350°F. Mix all ingredients, except Fritos®, in a 3-qt. dish then bake, uncovered approx. 30 mins. or until bubbly. Serve hot with Fritos®.

The Sweet Potato Queens' Guide to Raising Children for Fun and Profit
(Simon & Schuster, 2008), p. 85

QUEEN DIP

3 6-oz. jars artichoke hearts, drained

2 6-oz. cans crabmeat or

1 pkg. imitation crabmeat, chopped

2 8-oz. pkgs. Parmesan cheese, shredded

2 cups mayonnaise

½ cup cream cheese, softened

1/8 tsp. Salt

1/8 tsp. ground red pepper

Town House® crackers

Mix all ingredients, except crackers, in a microwave-safe dish and cook on *HIGH* in microwave for 5 mins., then stir it, and cook again for 5 mins. Serve with Town House® crackers.

The Sweet Potato Queens' Big-Ass Cookbook (and Financial Planner)
(Three Rivers Press, 2003), p. 208

QUEEN OF THE NIGHT SALSA

2 15-oz. cans black beans, rinsed and drained

1 17-oz. can whole kernel corn, drained

2 large tomatoes, peeled & chopped

1 purple onion, minced

1/8 to ¼ cup chopped fresh cilantro

4 TBSP lime juice

1 TBSP olive oil

1 TBSP red wine vinegar

1 tsp. salt

½ tsp. black pepper (or 1/8 tsp. red pepper)

1 large bag tortilla chips

Mix all ingredients, except chips, together and refrigerate for at least one hour before serving with tortilla chips and margaritas.

The Sweet Potato Queens' Big-Ass Cookbook (and Financial Planner)
(Three Rivers Press, 2003), p. 128

QUEEN OF THE NIGHT SALSA 2.0

1 15-oz. can black beans, rinsed and drained

1 11-oz. can Niblets® corn

1 4-oz. can chopped green chilis

1 small can chopped black olives

2-3 fresh tomatoes, peeled & chopped

8 ozs. Monterey Jack cheese, shredded (more if desired)

1 bunch green onions, chopped

½ tsp. chili powder

½ tsp. cumin

½ to ¾ bottle Wishbone® Robusto Italian Dressing®, 16 ozs.

1 lb. bacon, cooked, chopped

Chopped cilantro to taste — fresh or dried

1 large bag Fritos® Scoops

Mix all ingredients, except Fritos®, and chill in refrigerator overnight. Serve with Fritos® Scoops.

American Thighs:
The Sweet Potato Queens' Guide to Preserving Your Assets
(Simon & Schuster, 2009), p. 288

QUESO-PIG-ETARIAN DIP

2 11-oz. cans Mexican corn, drained

2 4-oz. cans chopped green chilis

1 small can chopped black olives

1 cup Hellman's® Real Mayonnaise

8 oz. Pepper Jack Cheese, shredded

1 lb. bacon, cooked, crumbled

1 large bag Fritos® Scoops.

Mix together all ingredients, except Fritos®, in a microwave-safe bowl then microwave until hot and bubbly. Top with bacon. Serve with Fritos® Scoops.

The Sweet Potato Queens' Big-Ass Cookbook (and Financial Planner)
(Three Rivers Press, 2003), p. 245

Spud Stud Scott-apeno Dip

8 ozs. sour cream

8 ozs. cream cheese, softened

1 jar Armour® dried beef, diced

1/3 – ½ cup diced jalapeños (canned or fresh)

1 bunch green onions, chopped

Paprika

1 large bag Fritos® Scoops or tortilla chips

Preheat oven to 350°F. Combine all ingredients, except Fritos®, in an appropriate-sized baking dish, sprinkle top with paprika and garnish with jalapeños slices, then bake for 30-45 mins. or until bubbly. Serve with tortilla chips or Fritos® Scoops.

*Freezes well.

(This is an up-dated version of the original published recipe.)

Fat Is The New 30:
The Sweet Potato Queens' Guide to Coping with (the crappy parts of) Life
(Amazon Publishing, 2012), p. 140

SPUD STUD SCOTT'S SAUSAGE BALLS*
(AND CHEESE GRITS)

1 lb. regular breakfast sausage

1 lb. hot breakfast sausage

2 cups shredded Sharp Cheddar cheese

2 cups shredded Pepper Jack cheese

1 TBSP Worcestershire sauce

4 cups Original Bisquick™ Pancake & Baking Mix

Preheat oven to 350°F. Combine all ingredients and mix thoroughly. Form into bite-sized balls (a melon baller works great). Bake on a greased cookie sheet for 15 mins. if to be served immediately.

For FREEZING: Bake for 13 minutes so they are formed and will not stick together in the freezer bag. They will not dry out when reheated.

To REHEAT: Put frozen sausage balls onto a greased cookie sheet then bake at 350°F for 15 mins.

*Excellent served with Cheese Grits for breakfast or as a stand-alone appetizer.

(Continues on the next page.)

Cheese Grits

Regular or Quick grits
(_never_ Instant)

Salted butter

Milk or cream

Sharp Cheddar cheese, shredded

Salt

Red pepper

Regular or Quick grits—_never_ Instant. Cook according to package directions. When grits are thickening, add butter, and milk or cream—enough of each to cause the grits to become thin again—and continue cooking over _LOW_ heat, stirring constantly until it begins to thicken again, then dump in copious amounts of Sharp Cheddar cheese. Salt and red pepper to taste.

This will one day appear in yet another _Sweet Potato Queens® book_, God willing.

SYLVIA'S CHEESE PETITS FOURS

3 loaves Pepperidge Farm® Very Thin White Bread

4 sticks salted butter

4 jars Kraft® Old English Spread

1½ tsp. Tabasco®

1 TBSP onion powder

½ tsp. cayenne

Preheat oven to 350°F. Cut crust off bread. Mix together butter, Kraft® Old English Spread, Tabasco®, onion power, and cayenne. Take three (3) slices of the crustless bread and spread the cheese mixture on each side and stack—then "ice" the stack with the mixture (like a cake) and cut the stack into four (4) pieces. Do this with all the bread and bake until crispy—about 15 to 20 mins. but watch closely. Don't over-brown. These freeze well (unbaked).

The Sweet Potato Queens' Big-Ass Cookbook (and Financial Planner)
(Three Rivers Press, 2003), p. 209

TAMMY DONNA'S KAY-SO DIP

1 lb. Pepper Jack or Manchego cheese, shredded

1 red bell pepper, chopped fine

½ lb. fresh baby spinach (more if desired)

2-3 medium tomatoes, peeled & chopped

1 quart milk

Bread, chips, or crackers

Melt cheese in top of double boiler then add bell pepper, spinach, and tomatoes and cook until spinach is wilted. Slowly add milk, stirring constantly. Continue cooking until mixture is hot. Serve hot with bread, chips, or crackers.

The Sweet Potato Queens' Field Guide to Men:
Every Man I Love is Either Married, Gay, or Dead
(Three Rivers Press, 2004), p. 215

THERE'S ALWAYS ROOM FOR BACON

Bacon (uncooked)

Club® or Waverly® crackers

Parmesan cheese, shredded

Preheat oven to 250°F. Cut bacon into thirds. Line a rimmed cookie sheet with foil. Place crackers on lined cookie sheet. Place bacon on top of each cracker. Sprinkle bacon liberally with Parmesan cheese. Bake for 2 hours. Remove from oven.

IMPORTANT:
Leave them ON THE COOKIE sheet until COMPLETELY cool.

Store at room temp in air-tight container. Do NOT refrigerate.

The Sweet Potato Queens' Field Guide to Men:
Every Man I Love is Either Married, Gay, or Dead
(Three Rivers Press, 2004), p. 220

DRINKS

80-PROOF CHERRY PIE
(AKA Tammy Georgia's 80-proof Cherry Pie)

1 glass

Zubrowka® Bison Brand Vodka

Apple Juice

In the glass, combine 1 part Zubrowka® and 2 parts apple juice. Tastes like cherry pie. No one knows why. No one cares why.

The Sweet Potato Queens' Guide to Raising Children for Fun and Profit
(Simon & Schuster, 2008), p. 86

ABSOLUT® FREDO
(AKA Re-Virginator™)

Absolut® Kurant*
Triple Sec
Rose's lime juice

For those who still have Kurant squirreled away: Mix together three (3) parts Absolut® Kurant, one (1) part Triple Sec, and one (1) part Rose's lime juice. All this is shaken over ice and served in a chilled martini glass.

*Since Absolut® quit making Kurant, Bravo! restaurant created:

ALMOST FREDO

1.5 ozs. Absolut® Berri Açaí
1 oz. Triple Sec
½ oz. lime juice
Splash Simple Syrup
Twist of lime

Combine, shaken over ice; served in chilled martini glass. Garnish with twist of lime.

The Sweet Potato Queens Book of Love
(Three Rivers Press, 1999), p. 175

and

The Sweet Potato Queens' Big-Ass Cookbook (and Financial Planner)
(Three Rivers Press, 2003), p. 256

DON'T ASK ME AGAIN FOR THE PINEAPPLE VODKA RECIPE

8 to 10 20-oz. cans *juice*-packed, pineapple rings, drained

1 liter (*good*) vodka

Put the drained pineapple rings into a large sealable container and pour the vodka over them. Seal the container and refrigerate for seven (7) days. On the 8th day, drain just the vodka into a large enough container or a sealable pitcher for transport to the pool or the lake. Shake the vodka over ice and serve in a chilled martini glass if indoors or stemless drinkware suitable for outdoor use.

American Thighs:
The Sweet Potato Queens' Guide to Preserving Your Assets
(Simon & Schuster, 2009), p. 288

New Allison's Mambo Margaritas

1 12-oz. can frozen limeade

1 bottle Corona® beer

12 ozs. Seven-Up®

12 ozs. really good tequila

In a large pitcher, pour in limeade then beer. Add Seven-Up® (never Sprite®) then tequila. **Stir.**

Do NOT attempt to mix this in a blender.

We've blown off the tops of blenders, spraying this sticky mess all over our respective kitchens.

The Sweet Potato Queens Book of Love
(Three Rivers Press, 1999), p. 173

and

The Sweet Potato Queens' Big-Ass Cookbook (and Financial Planner)
(Three Rivers Press, 2003), p. 256

Re-Virginator™
(AKA Absolut® Fredo)

Absolut® Kurant*

Triple Sec

Rose's lime juice

For those who still have Kurant squirreled away: Mix together three (3) parts Absolut® Kurant, one (1) part Triple Sec, and one (1) part Rose's lime juice. All this is shaken over ice and served in a chilled martini glass.

*Since Absolut® quit making Kurant, Bravo! restaurant created:

Almost Fredo

1.5 ozs. Absolut® Berri Açaí

1 oz. Triple Sec

½ oz. lime juice

Splash Simple Syrup

Twist of lime

Combine, shaken over ice; served in chilled martini glass. Garnish with twist of lime.

The Sweet Potato Queens Book of Love
(Three Rivers Press, 1999), p. 175

and

The Sweet Potato Queens' Big-Ass Cookbook (and Financial Planner)
(Three Rivers Press, 2003), p. 256

Slushy, Lushy Lemonade

1 fifth Southern Comfort® (80 or 100 proof)

6 ozs. frozen lemonade concentrate

6 ozs. frozen orange juice concentrate

1 2-liter citrus soda

Combine all ingredients in a sealable pitcher and freeze to desired slushy consistency.

The Sweet Potato Queens' Wedding Planner and Divorce Guide
(Crown Publishers, 2007), *Divorce Guide* side, p. 115

TAMMY GEORGIA'S 80-PROOF CHERRY PIE
(AKA 80-Proof Cherry Pie)

1 glass

Zubrowka® Bison Brand Vodka

Apple Juice

In the glass, combine 1 part Zubrowka® and 2 parts apple juice. Tastes like cherry pie. No one knows why. No one cares why. It just do.

The Sweet Potato Queens' Guide to Raising Children for Fun and Profit
(Simon & Schuster, 2008), p. 86

TINY-WEENY WOO-WOO

1 64-oz. bottle cran-grape juice

1½ cups peach schnapps

1 cup orange juice

Vodka—optional

In a sealable pitcher, combine all ingredients. Can be frozen to "slushy" consistency, if desired. Good with or without vodka to your taste/tolerance. Works well as a punch with orange and lemon slices for garnish.

Fat Is The New 30:
The Sweet Potato Queens' Guide to Coping with (the crappy parts of) Life
(Amazon Publishing, 2012), p. 146

TROUBLE MONKEY

Absolut® Mandarin vodka

Cranberry juice

7-UP®

Juice of one-half orange

In a sealable pitcher, mix 3 parts vodka, 2 parts cranberry juice, 1 part 7-UP®, and the orange juice. Add the mashed-up orange to the mix to eat later.

The Sweet Potato Queens' Big-Ass Cookbook (and Financial Planner)
(Three Rivers Press, 2003), p. 27

MEAT

ALMOST IMMEDIATELY DELICIOUS
PORK TENDERLOINS IN AN INSTANT POT®

1-3 pork TENDERLOINS (_not_ pork loin)

Salt and pepper to taste

Garlic powder

Italian seasoning

Sauce

4 TBSP soy sauce

1 cup dark brown sugar

½ cup balsamic vinegar

1 cup chicken broth

½–1 tsp. liquid smoke (optional)

Slurry

2–4 TBSP corn starch

Water

Cut each tenderloin into two pieces so that they will fit into your Instant Pot® (mine is 8-quarts). Sprinkle all of the seasonings on all sides of the pork.

(Continues on the next page.)

Mix well all of the Sauce ingredients in a bowl then pour Sauce into your Instant Pot®. Put meat directly into the bottom of the pot. (Some pieces will be stacked.)

Set to *Pressure Cook* for three (3) mins. Allow pressure to release naturally. Meat will be just barely pink—perfectly cooked. No need to increase cooking time for multiple tenderloins.

Remove meat. Pour Sauce from the Instant Pot® into a small sauce pan, set on *MEDIUM* heat.

Create a Slurry in a cup or small a bowl by combining corn starch with just enough cold water to dissolve it. (Make a small amount of Slurry to start.) Put the Slurry into the heated Sauce and stir constantly until it thickens to the desired consistency. Make more Slurry if necessary.

Serve meat with Sauce.

This will one day appear in yet another *Sweet Potato Queens® book*, God willing.

Bitch Meatballs with Sexy Red Sauce

2 lbs. ground chuck

1 TBSP salt

1 lb. ground pork

2½ cups Italian bread crumbs

4 tsp. garlic, chopped

1 cup Parmesan cheese

1 cup parsley, chopped

6 eggs

3 slices bread (soaked in water and squeezed out)

4 TBSP olive oil

½ teaspoon black pepper

Vegetable oil

Combine all ingredients (except for vegetable oil) in large bowl. With wet hands, roll into balls (ping pong size)—don't over-compact. Heat vegetable oil (enough for browning purposes only) in skillet then brown meatballs on all sides. No need to cook through—they will complete cooking in the…

(Continues on the next page.)

Sexy Red Sauce

Pork or beef ribs or small bone-in steak

Olive oil

2 28-oz. cans whole Italian tomatoes

2 6-oz. cans Italian tomato paste

1 15-oz. can tomato puree

28 ozs. water

2 TBSP sugar

2 tsp. EACH oregano, basil, thyme

4 TBSP beef base

½ cup fresh parsley, chopped

10 "shakes" regular Mrs. Dash®
(or whatever they call it these days)

½ cup red wine

1 medium onion, peeled & chopped

1 whole head fresh garlic, peeled & chopped

3 TBSP olive oil

Brown the meat in enough olive oil to coat bottom of large stock pot and remove from skillet. Add tomatoes, paste, puree, and water. Blend thoroughly.

(Continues on the next page.)

Add sugar, spices, beef base, parsley, Mrs. Dash®, and wine. Cook over *MEDIUM* heat, uncovered.

In skillet, lightly brown onion and garlic in olive oil. Add to stock pot and continue cooking at least 2 hours, stirring frequently, tasting often. Add meatballs and cook until done through—at least an hour. Add water as needed to keep sauce consistency of motor oil. Salt and pepper to taste.

The Sweet Potato Queens' Big-Ass Cookbook (and Financial Planner)
(Three Rivers Press, 2003), p. 201

DREAMY CREAMY PORK LOIN

1 4-5 lb. pork loin

2 cups heavy cream

3-4 slices bacon (uncooked)

Kosher salt

Cut pork loin in half, lengthwise. Sprinkle with Kosher salt. Put in Crock-Pot® and top with bacon slices. Pour cream over pork, lifting to be sure it is underneath as well. Cook on *LOW* for 3½ hours. Meat should be very slightly pink but not translucent. DO NOT OVER-COOK. Serve topped with the cream from the pot. Freezes well.

Watch cooking time—over-cooked pork is ruined pork and that is tragic.

This will one day appear in yet another *Sweet Potato Queens® book*, God willing.

JEWISH BARBECUE

1 slab brisket (NOT corned beef)

1 jar Heinz® Chili Sauce

1 can whole-berry cranberry sauce

Combine sauces and pour over brisket in Crock-Pot®. Cook on *LOW* for 6-8 hours.

The Sweet Potato Queens' First Big-Ass Novel:
Stuff we didn't actually do, but could have, and may yet
(Simon & Schuster, 2008), p. 283

LANCE ROMANCE AND THE LUSCIOUS PIG

Pork—can be sliced loin, sliced tenderloin*, or chops

½ cup soy sauce

½ cup sugar (or Splenda®)

2 or 3 garlic cloves, minced

Combine soy, sugar, and garlic in a large Ziploc-type bag. Add pork and put in refrigerator overnight—or even several days. Take out and arrange on rimmed cookie sheet. Put in oven on BROIL for 3-7 mins. per side, depending on the thickness of meat. It cooks very quickly—don't overcook.

*If using pork loin or tenderloin, have the butcher slice it very thin.

The Sweet Potato Queens' Big-Ass Cookbook (and Financial Planner)
(Three Rivers Press, 2003), p. 236

MEAT AND 'MATERS

3½ lbs. round steak

Bacon (uncooked)

¼ tsp. EACH black pepper, red pepper, salt

1/3 cup salted butter

1½ TBSP dark brown sugar

3 cups tomatoes (canned or fresh)

1¼ cups water

Cut lengthwise pockets in steak and put slice of bacon inside. Combine seasonings and rub on surface of steak. Melt butter in iron skillet and brown meat on both sides. Add sugar, tomatoes, and water. Cover pan, reduce heat to *LOW* and *Simmer* for 90 mins. or until tender.

The Sweet Potato Queens' Field Guide to Men:
Every Man I Love is Either Married, Gay, or Dead
(Three Rivers Press, 2004), p. 213

SUCCULENT BEEF DISH OF MY NEXT HUSBAND
(AKA Suculentos Platos de Carne de Vacuno de Mi Proximo Marido)
(Adapted with permission from Robert St. John's: *Deep South Staples*)

2 2½ to 3 lb. shoulder roasts

¼ cup bacon grease or canola oil

Kosher salt, garlic powder, onion powder

¼ cup olive oil

½ cup flour

1 bag frozen chopped onions

¼ tsp. thyme

3 cups hot beef broth

2 tsp. Worcestershire sauce

1 tsp. salt

1 TBSP tomato paste (optional)

Season meat on all sides with Kosher salt, garlic, and onion powder. Heat grease in skillet and brown meat on all sides then transfer to Crock-Pot®. Lower heat on skillet, add olive oil and stir in flour—cook, stirring constantly, to make peanut-butter colored roux. Add onions and thyme—cook for 4-5 mins. Add beef broth, Worcestershire, salt, and tomato paste. Stir until well-blended then pour over the roasts. Cook on *LOW* setting for several hours. (Slow cookers vary—test for desired doneness with your cooker.)

(Continues on the next page.)

NOTE: If gravy is too thin when done, pour it off into a sauce pan over *LOW* heat. Dissolve 3-4 TBSP cornstarch in just enough water to make smooth and pour into gravy. Stir constantly until gravy is desired consistency.

Freezes very well.

American Thighs:
The Sweet Potato Queens' Guide to Preserving Your Assets
(Simon & Schuster, 2009), p. 293

Suculentos Platos de Carne de Vacuno de Mi Proximo Marido
(AKA Succulent Beef Dish of my Next Husband)
(Adapted with permission from Robert St. John's: *Deep South Staples*)

2 2½ to 3 lb. shoulder roasts

¼ cup bacon grease or canola oil

Kosher salt, garlic powder, onion powder

¼ cup olive oil

½ cup flour

1 bag frozen chopped onions

¼ tsp. thyme

3 cups hot beef broth

2 tsp. Worcestershire sauce

1 tsp. salt

1 TBSP tomato paste (optional)

Season meat on all sides with Kosher salt, garlic, and onion powder. Heat grease in skillet and brown meat on all sides then transfer to Crock-Pot®. Lower heat on skillet, add olive oil and stir in flour—cook, stirring constantly, to make peanut-butter colored roux. Add onions and thyme—cook for 4-5 mins. Add beef broth, Worcestershire, salt, and tomato paste. Stir until well-blended then pour over the roasts. Cook on *LOW* setting for several hours. (Slow cookers vary—test for desired doneness with your cooker.)

(Continues on the next page.)

NOTE: If gravy is too thin when done, pour it off into a sauce pan over *LOW* heat. Dissolve 3-4 TBSP cornstarch in just enough water to make smooth and pour into gravy. Stir constantly until gravy is desired consistency.

Freezes very well.

American Thighs:
The Sweet Potato Queens' Guide to Preserving Your Assets
(Simon & Schuster, 2009), p. 293

THE GREAT SMOKEY'S CREMATED TENDERLOIN

1 beef tenderloin, trimmed*

1 stick salted butter

½ cup Pompeian olive oil

¼ cup white vinegar

Juice of two (2) lemons

2 heaping TBSP sugar

3 heaping tsp. dried parsley flakes

2 tsp. Worcestershire sauce

Water

Salt, garlic powder, crushed pepper to taste

Mix all ingredients, except the tenderloin, in a large pot and bring to *Boil*. Put tenderloin in pot and allow to *Boil* 2 mins. Cool, cover and refrigerate for 1-2 days.

Build a *hot fire* on a grill with a lid. Place tenderloin on grill and cook for 8 mins. on first side, "even if it looks like it is being cremated." Turn and cook 5 mins. Remove if Rare meat is preferred. Cook slightly longer for Medium Rare. "*Please do not cook Well Done.*"

*If you purchase a whole beef tenderloin from a genuine butcher, have him/her trim it for you and grind the trimmings for the best hamburgers you ever had in your life.

(Continues on the next page.)

This is the prized recipe of our dear, departed friend James E. "Smokey" Davis, Jr. from Mauvilla, Alabama, who did so love to be mentioned in any way in every book I write—so here you go, Smoke! The quotes are directly from him. He is much-loved and so very much-missed.

This will one day appear in yet another *Sweet Potato Queens® book*, God willing.

TINY BUT POWERFUL GRIEF-RELIEVING MEAT LOAVES

1 egg

¼ cup milk

1 cup barbecue sauce

1½ stalks celery, chopped fine

½ cup salsa

½ bell pepper, chopped fine

1½ TBSP Worcestershire sauce

1 medium onion, chopped fine

¼ tsp. ground red pepper

1 cup bread crumbs

¼ tsp. salt

1½ lbs. ground round or sirloin

Preheat oven to 450°F. Mix egg with milk. Add vegetables, bread crumbs, meat, and salt. Mix well. In another bowl, mix barbecue sauce, salsa, Worcestershire, red pepper, and salt. Stir half that sauce into the meat mixture. Put ½ cup meat mix into each well of a Texas-sized muffin pan or a mini loaf pan. Top each with remaining sauce. Bake 18-20 mins. These freeze well and also make fantastic sandwiches.

The Sweet Potato Queens' First Big-Ass Novel:
Stuff we didn't actually do, but could have, and may yet
(Simon & Schuster, 2008), p. 281

WHO CROAKED? CROCK-POT® PORK

1 16-oz. can whole berry cranberry sauce

1 medium onion, chopped

1 5.5 oz. can apricot nectar

½ cup sugar (or Splenda®)

½ cup dried apricots, chopped

2 tsp. white vinegar

1 tsp. dry mustard

1 tsp. salt

¼ to ½ tsp. crushed red pepper

2½ lbs. boneless pork loin

Mix all ingredients together in Crock-Pot® and pour over pork. If time permits, refrigerate overnight but can be cooked right away. Cook on *LOW* for several hours until desired doneness. Don't overcook — pork should be slightly pink.

The Sweet Potato Queens' 1ˢᵗ Big-Ass Novel:
Stuff we didn't actually do, but could have, and may yet
(Simon & Schuster, 2008), p. 280

SALADS

BROCCOLI SALAD

1 bunch broccoli, florets only, chopped

1 small red onion, chopped very fine

½ cup raisins

2/3 cup mayo

¼ cup sugar (or Splenda®)

2 tsp. white vinegar

8 slices bacon (minimum) cooked and crumbled

Put broccoli, onion and raisins in a mixing bowl. Combine mayo, sugar (or Splenda®), and vinegar, mixing well. Pour over the broccoli mixture and toss until well-coated. Refrigerate for at least 2 hours. Right before serving, add the crumbled bacon and toss.

The Sweet Potato Queens' Big-Ass Cookbook (and Financial Planner)
(Three Rivers Press, 2003), p. 212

DAMON LEE FOWLER'S POTATO SALAD — REINCARNATED
(Damon Lee Fowler's recipe; used with permission.)

Leftover potato salad

½ cup salted butter

1 cup plain bread crumbs or

Ritz® cracker crumbs or potato chip crumbs

Preheat oven to 400°F. Put potato salad into an appropriate-sized baking dish. Melt butter, stir in bread or Ritz® crumbs. (If using potato chip crumbs, omit butter.) Put crumbs on top of potato salad and bake for 25-30 mins. Serve hot.

The Sweet Potato Queens' First Big-Ass Novel:
Stuff we didn't actually do, but could have, and may yet
(Simon & Schuster, 2008), p. 288

HAL & MAL'S COME BACK SAUCE

2 cups mayo

½ cup ketchup

1 cup canola oil

2 TBSP black pepper

Juice of 2 lemons

2 tsp. yellow mustard

2 tsp. Worcestershire sauce

½ onion, grated

2 dashes Tabasco®

Dump all ingredients into food processor and blend until smooth. Refrigerate.

The Sweet Potato Queens Book of Love
(Three Rivers Press, 1999), p. 177

and

The Sweet Potato Queens' Big-Ass Cookbook (and Financial Planner)
(Three Rivers Press, 2003), p. 257

Highest & Best Use of Chili-Cheese Fritos® Salad

1 can whole kernel corn, drained

1 11-oz. can Green Giant® SteamCrisp® Mexicorn®, drained

½ cup mayo

½ cup Sharp Cheddar cheese, shredded

2 TBSP salsa

2 to 3 green onions, chopped

1 bag (~9.25 oz.) Chili-Cheese Fritos®

Combine all ingredients, except Fritos®, in a mixing bowl and chill in fridge for a few hours. Right before serving, mix in ½ bag (or so) Chili-Cheese Fritos®. May crush or leave whole — whole is highly recommended.

This will one day appear in yet another *Sweet Potato Queens®* book, God willing.

In Theory, I Hate This Chicken Salad

1 cup mayo

½ cup mango chutney (more to taste)

1 tsp. curry powder

8 chicken breasts, cooked, chopped

2 stalks celery, chopped

½ cup Vidalia onion, chopped*

2 Granny Smith apples, peeled & chopped

½ cup pecans, toasted, chopped

½ cup red grapes, halved (more to taste)

Mix mayo, chutney and curry powder. Combine chicken, celery, onion, apples, pecans and grapes in a mixing bowl. Pour the mayo mixture over it and toss thoroughly.

*If Vidalia or other "sweet" onions are not in season, chop a yellow onion and sprinkle a little Splenda® over it—not as good but a reasonable substitute.

Fat Is The New 30:
The Sweet Potato Queens' Guide to Coping with (the crappy parts of) Life
(Amazon Publishing, 2012), p. 138

KATHY'S
NOBODY-ELSE-IN-VENICE-BEACH-COOKS-LIKE-THIS
JELL-O®

1 8-oz. pkg. cream cheese, chopped and softened

1 3-oz. pkg. lime Jell-O®

1 3-oz. pkg. lemon Jell-O®

1 14-oz. can Eagle Brand® Sweetened Condensed Milk

1 20-oz. can crushed pineapple

1 (heaping) tsp. mayo

Mix up Jell-O® according to package directions then stir in softened cream cheese pieces, mashing the cream cheese into even smaller bits as you stir. Add remaining ingredients, pour into Bundt pan (or any mold) and refrigerate until set.

The Sweet Potato Queens' Big-Ass Cookbook (and Financial Planner)
(Three Rivers Press, 2003), p. 50

LOU'S SLAW

4 TBSP sugar (or Splenda®)

6 TBSP white vinegar

1 16-oz. pkg. unprepared coleslaw

1 cup canola oil

½ tsp. black pepper

1 tsp. salt

1 tsp. Tony Chachere's® Seasoning

2 3-oz. pkgs. chicken ramen noodles (crushed)

1 cup pecans, chopped

¼ cup onions, finely chopped

Heat vinegar and sugar together until sugar is melted. (No need to heat if using Splenda®—it dissolves instantly.) Mix together all other ingredients in large bowl and pour the vinegar/sugar over it and toss until completely blended. For best results, chill in refrigerator overnight.

The Sweet Potato Queens' Big-Ass Cookbook (and Financial Planner)
(Three Rivers Press, 2003), p. 213

PROMISED LAND PASTA SALAD

4 cups Rotini pasta, cooked *al dente*

1 4-oz. jar pimentos, drained

1 2-oz. can sliced, black olives, drained

½ cup chopped onion

¾ sugar (or Splenda®)

½ cup white vinegar

¼ cup canola oil

½ tsp. crushed red pepper

Mix together pasta, pimentos, black olives, and onion. Separately, mix sugar or Splenda®, oil and red pepper. (Note: if using sugar, mixture will have to be heated slightly to dissolve sugar. No need with Splenda®.) Pour over pasta mixture and toss well.

VARIATION: Omit raw onion from above. Grill and chop 1 lb. fresh asparagus, 1 or two Vidalia onions, and some GOOD tomatoes (use cherry tomatoes if the regular ones are not in season.) To grill, coat lightly with oil and use an open grill basket—adding tomatoes for last few minutes only. Toss the grilled veggies in with all the above. Chopped grilled chicken breast is also good in this.

The Sweet Potato Queens' First Big-Ass Novel:
Stuff we didn't actually do, but could have, and may yet
(Simon & Schuster, 2008), p. 280

REDNECK SALAD

2 boxes JIFFY® cornbread mix

1 lb. bacon, fried & crumbled

½ cup dill pickle juice

1½ cups mayo

1 Vidalia onion, chopped fine*

1 green, bell pepper, chopped fine

2 tomatoes, diced

Make cornbread according to package; when cool, crumble into bite-size chunks and set aside. Fry 1 lb. bacon and let cool. Whisk together dill juice, mayo, onion, pepper, and tomatoes. In a large bowl, layer 1/3 of the cornbread, follow with layer of dressing, and repeat until all used. Top with crumbled bacon. Needs to sit in refrigerator for at least one hour before serving—overnight is best.

*If Vidalia or other "sweet" onions are not in season, chop a yellow onion and sprinkle a little Splenda® over it—not as good but a reasonable substitute.

Fat Is The New 30:
The Sweet Potato Queens' Guide to Coping with (the crappy parts of) Life
(Amazon Publishing, 2012), p. 143

SHAMEFUL SECRET SALAD

1 8-oz. container Cool-Whip®

3 apples, peeled & diced

3 regular size Snickers® bars, frozen

Stir apple pieces into Cool-Whip®. Before unwrapping frozen Snickers® bars, smash them with a kitchen mallet. Stir the fragments into the Cool-Whip® mixture. Let sit at room temp for 15-20 mins.

Fat Is The New 30:
The Sweet Potato Queens' Guide to Coping with (the crappy parts of) Life
(Amazon Publishing, 2012), p. 147

SAMMICHES

BEANIE SAMMICHES
(AKA Beta Mom's Fabulous Beanie Sammiches)

10 or 12 boneless, skinless chicken thighs

4 28-oz. cans Bush's® Best Original Baked Beans

3 cups chopped onion

2 cups McClard's® Bar-B-Q Sauce

2 TBSP French's yellow mustard

2 tsp. chili powder

2 tsp. sugar (substitute Splenda®)

2 tsp. salt

Dump all of the ingredients into your big-ass Crock-Pot®. Cover then cook on *HIGH* for 5 to 6 hours or *LOW* for 8 to 12 hours. Take the chicken out, cut into bite-sized chunks and put it back in. (Depending on how much liquid was released by the chicken—sometimes it's a little too "soupy." If so, dump it all into a big pot and cook it for a few minutes on the stove, over *MEDIUM* heat, uncovered, until it cooks down to suit you, stir often.) Serve on split hamburger buns—but you'll have to eat it with a fork because it's *reeeal* messy. (½ the ingredients for a small Crock-Pot®.)

The Sweet Potato Queens' Guide to Raising Children for Fun and Profit
(Simon & Schuster, 2008), p. 80

BEER AND A SAMMICH

2 slices/slabs sourdough bread

Salted butter

Good bleu cheese dressing

Provolone or Pepper Jack cheese

Several roast beef slices

Beer

Thoroughly butter one slice/slab sourdough bread. Place it butter-side down on the grill and put your cheese choice on top and then put roast beef slices on top of that. Take the other hunk of sourdough and slather on a bunch of really *good* bleu cheese dressing on one side of it and a bunch of butter on the other side. Place it bleu-cheese-side down on top of the grilling sammich. When the cheese inside looks melty, flip it over and grill it on the other side. When it's toasted on that side, remove it from the grill, slap it on a plate, pop a top, and enjoy.

The Sweet Potato Queens' Field Guide to Men:
Every Man I Love is Either Married, Gay, or Dead
(Three Rivers Press, 2004), p. 219

Beta Mom's Fabulous Beanie Sammiches
(AKA Beanie Sammiches)

10 or 12 boneless, skinless chicken thighs

4 28-oz. cans Bush's® Best Original Baked Beans

3 cups chopped onion

2 cups McClard's® Bar-B-Q Sauce

2 TBSP French's yellow mustard

2 tsp. chili powder

2 tsp. sugar (substitute Splenda®)

2 tsp. salt

Dump all of the ingredients into your big-ass Crock-Pot®. Cover then cook on *HIGH* for 5 to 6 hours or *LOW* for 8 to 12 hours. Take the chicken out, cut into bite-sized chunks and put it back in. (Depending on how much liquid was released by the chicken—sometimes it's a little too "soupy." If so, dump it all into a big pot and cook it for a few minutes on the stove, over *MEDIUM* heat, uncovered, until it cooks down to suit you, stir often.) Serve on split hamburger buns—but you'll have to eat it with a fork because it's *reeeal* messy. (½ the ingredients for a small Crock-Pot®.)

The Sweet Potato Queens' Guide to Raising Children for Fun and Profit
(Simon & Schuster, 2008), p. 80

GRILLED BOLOGNA PO-BOY

High-quality bologna, sliced thick*

Purple onion, sliced

Pepper Jack cheese

Sharp Cheddar cheese

French bread

***Do NOT use pre-sliced bologna.
Get the whole sausage and cut thick slices.**

Cook bologna slices and onion slices—using either an open grill basket or a closed grill basket—on your grill until the onions are tender. Melt Pepper Jack and Cheddar on bread slices. Add bologna and onions. Eat.

The Sweet Potato Queens' Big-Ass Cookbook (and Financial Planner)
(Three Rivers Press, 2003), p. 61

ONLY SLIGHTLY SINFUL SAUSAGE SUB

1 long loaf *good* French bread

1 lb. Bryan® sausage, hot or mild

Pepper Jack cheese, slices

½ cup chopped onion

1 cup chopped celery

2 eggs

¼ cup milk

1 tsp. ground sage

1/8 tsp. black pepper

1 stick salted butter

Slice off the top 1/3 of the French bread loaf. Hollow out the lower section and tear the excess bread into little pieces. In an iron skillet brown sausage and drain off fat. Add onion and celery to the sausage and cook until tender. In a mixing bowl, combine eggs, milk, sage, and black pepper. Dump the bread pieces into that and stir it all up until the bread is coated. Dump the sausage stuff into that and stir it all up. Melt butter and brush all of it inside the top and bottom of the bread boat. Put the bottom of the boat on a giant sheet of foil and then fill it with the sausage goo. Overlap goo with slices of cheese. Put the top on and tightly wrap the whole thing in foil. Cool in the fridge overnight. Bring to room temp, then heat it for 40 minutes at 320 degrees. (Straight out of the fridge takes about 55 mins. to heat.)

(Continues on the next page.)

ALTERNATIVE: Break an egg into a microwave-safe mug, cover with plastic wrap if it doesn't have a lid, then zap it for about 40 secs. Cut off a hunk of the Sub, lift the top and slide your egg on top of the cheese, replace the top and chow down.

Fat Is The New 30:
The Sweet Potato Queens' Guide to Coping with (the crappy parts of) Life
(Amazon Publishing, 2012), p. 145

PASSION FOR PIMIENTO
(Damon Lee Fowler's Recipe; used with permission.)

2 cups Extra-Sharp Cheddar cheese, shredded

½ cup Parmigiano-Reggiano cheese, grated

5-6 heaping TBSP mayonnaise

1 4-oz. jar pimientos, drain and reserve juice

Cayenne pepper to taste

Dump ingredients into a bowl and mix with your hands—add pimiento juice as needed for desired consistency.

The Sweet Potato Queens' First Big-Ass Novel:
Stuff we didn't actually do, but could have, and may yet
(Simon & Schuster, 2008), p. 286

VINEY'S FLOOR-OF-THE-HILTON® MINNER CHEESE*

1 lb. Kraft Cracker Barrel® Sharp Cheddar cheese, grated * *

1 small onion, finely minced

1 4-oz. jar pimientos

1 cup Hellman's® Real Mayonnaise

Red pepper (optional)

Combine all ingredients in a mixing bowl—add more mayo if desired.

*So named because of where it is consumed. (The mentioned Hilton® is the Hilton-Jackson, on County Line Road in Jackson, Mississippi—O-fficial Home of THE Sweet Potato Queens®.)

* * Do NOT substitute pre-shredded cheese. Get the block of Cracker Barrel® and grate it or shred in food processor.

Fat Is The New 30:
The Sweet Potato Queens' Guide to Coping with (the crappy parts of) Life
(Amazon Publishing, 2012), p. 145.

The Sweet Potato Queens'
BIG-ASS COMPENDIUM OF FAT & HAPPY

179

WHY-OMING CHEESE HOUSE MINNER CHEESE

1 lb. Extra-Sharp Cheddar cheese, shredded

½ lb. Pepper Jack cheese, shredded

1 cup Duke's® or Hellman's® Real Mayonnaise

1 4.5-oz. can chopped green chilis

1 medium Poblano pepper, seeded and chopped

1 4-oz. jar pimientos

¼ cup sweet onion, chopped fine

2 tsp. Worcestershire sauce

Combine all ingredients in food processor and blend until desired consistency. Serve on crackers or white bread, crusts removed.

The Sweet Potato Queens' Big-Ass Cookbook (and Financial Planner)
(Three Rivers Press, 2003), p. 178

SEAFOOD

ARMADILLO HUNTERS' SHRIMP

1 tsp. anise seeds

1 tsp. cumin seeds

2 TBSP vegetable oil

4 scallions, coarsely chopped

2 cloves garlic, minced

¾ lb. plum tomatoes, coarsely chopped

2 medium jalapeño peppers, cut in rings

1 tsp. oregano

1 tsp. pepper

½ tsp. salt

1 lb. medium shrimp, peeled

Lime wedges

Rice w/cilantro or saffron rice

(Continues on the next page.)

In a large, stainless steel skillet, toast anise and cumin seeds over *MEDIUM* heat—remove and reserve. Heat oil until smoking and cook scallions and garlic over *HIGH* heat, just until soft (about 2 mins.). Add tomatoes, jalapeños, oregano, pepper, and salt—cook for 2 mins. Stir in shrimp, cook, stirring occasionally, until shrimp turn pink. Serve with lime wedges, over rice cooked with cilantro in the water—or saffron rice.

The Sweet Potato Queens' Big-Ass Cookbook (and Financial Planner)
(Three Rivers Press, 2003), p. 226

BITCH BAR™ BACON SWIMPS

Thin-sliced bacon

Fresh shrimp, large

Pepper Jack cheese

Barbecue sauce
(Sweet, hot variety such as McClard's®)

Microwave bacon until NEARLY done. Peel, de-vein, and butterfly shrimp. Put a hunk of Pepper Jack in the butterflied shrimp and wrap each in a piece of nearly-cooked bacon. Grill using either an open grill basket or a closed grill basket until the shrimp turns pink and the bacon finishes cooking. Right before removing shrimp from the grill, slather each with your favorite sweet, hot barbecue sauce. Allow to cool slightly before eating.

**Caution:
Cheese is molten lava-like!**

The Sweet Potato Queens' Big-Ass Cookbook (and Financial Planner)
(Three Rivers Press, 2003), p. 79

JUDY'S CRAWFISH MONICA

1½ lbs. Rotini pasta, cooked *al dente*

1 cup salted butter

3 TBSP Cajun seasoning

1½ quarts heavy cream

1 cup green onions, chopped

1½ lbs. crawfish tail meat

Melt butter in a deep iron skillet until bubbly. Stir in Cajun seasoning and blend well. Add the cream—cook until reduced by half. Add green onions and crawfish tail meat. Cook until heated through. (Crawfish tails are sold parboiled.) Add the pasta and toss well.

The Sweet Potato Queens' Big-Ass Cookbook (and Financial Planner)
(Three Rivers Press, 2003), p. 95

OUR DADDY'S CRAWFISH ÉTOUFFÉE

15 TBSP oil, divided

5 TBSP flour

3 medium onions, chopped

2 medium bell peppers, chopped

2½ quarts water, divided

8 cups peeled crawfish tails (or shrimp)

1½ tsp. salt

½ tsp. red pepper

Rice

Put 5 TBSP oil in an 8-qt. heavy pot — add onions, peppers, and seasonings. Cook, stirring frequently, over *LOW* heat until onions are translucent. Add 2 qts. water, allow to *Simmer* while you make the roux.

Make a roux: Put 10 TBSP oil and flour in an iron skillet, cook, stirring constantly over *LOW* heat until brown. This is a SLOW process that cannot be rushed. Keep stirring and do NOT burn it.

When the roux is brown, stir in remaining pint of water; stir until smooth then add to onion/pepper mixture, cooking over *LOW* heat for about 2½ hours, until thick. Add crawfish in final 15 mins. of cooking.

Serve over rice — with hot sauce on the side.

The Sweet Potato Queens' Big-Ass Cookbook (and Financial Planner)
(Three Rivers Press, 2003), p. 85.

SOUPS & STEWS

ARMAGEDDON STEW

1 can beef, shredded

1 can pork, shredded

1 can chicken, shredded

3 cans creamed corn

2 cans stewed tomatoes

½ cup white vinegar

1 medium onion, chopped

Salt

Pepper

Rice

Combine all ingredients in a Crock-Pot® and cook on *LOW* for 10-24 hours. (May substitute fresh, cooked meats and chicken, if it's not TEOTWAWKI*.) Salt and pepper to taste.

Serve over rice.

*The End of the World as We Know It.

Fat Is The New 30:
The Sweet Potato Queens' Guide to Coping with (the crappy parts of) Life
(Amazon Publishing, 2012), p. 148

CHEESE SOUP FOR MY BELOVED PASTOR
(AKA Sopa de Queso para mi Amado Pastor)

½ cup salted butter

1 cup chopped onion

1 cup grated carrot

1 cup celery, chopped fine

½ cup flour

8 cups heavy cream

8 cups chicken broth

¼ tsp. baking soda

6 jars Kraft® Old English Cheese or 8 cups shredded cheese
(Sharp Cheddar or Cheddar with habaneros)

Paprika or cayenne

In an 8-qt. heavy pot, cook vegetables in butter until very tender. Stir in flour, mix well. Add cream, chicken broth, baking soda and cheese. Cook, stirring, over *LOW* heat until cheese is melted. Serve sprinkled with either paprika or cayenne.

This will one day appear in yet another *Sweet Potato Queens® book*, God willing.

CHICKEN, ANDOUILLE, AND OYSTER GUMBO

3 lbs. chicken thighs

4 cups water/chicken broth
(may sub chicken broth for ½ or all, optional)

½ cup flour

½ cup oil or bacon grease

1½ cup yellow onion, chopped

1½ cup celery, chopped

½ cup green bell pepper, chopped

½ cup green onion, chopped

3 cloves garlic, pressed

¼ cup parsley, chopped

1 bay leaf

½ tsp. thyme

1 lb. okra, cut (may use frozen)

¾ lb. Andouille or smoked sausage, sliced

Salt, pepper, cayenne, Worcestershire sauce to taste

1 cup oysters with liquid (optional)

3 cups steamed rice

Cook chicken in water/broth until tender. Skim top for fat and foam. Remove chicken, cool, take off skin and debone, then cut into bite-size chunks. Reserve stock.

(Continues on the next page.)

FYI: the best tasting stock is made with bone-in/skin-on chicken, cooked in chicken broth.

MAKE A ROUX: Put the oil and flour into an 8-qt. heavy pot, cook, stirring constantly over *LOW* heat until brown. (Don't rush—this is not quick. Do not burn it.)

When roux is ready, add the vegetables, garlic, parsley, bay leaf, and thyme. Cook until tender, stirring often. Slowly add stock and then chicken meat.

In an iron skillet, fry sausage to remove fat, drain well and add to gumbo pot. Cover and *SIMMER* one (1) hour, stirring occasionally. Taste and season to preference. If desired, add oysters with liquid then heat just until oysters' edges curl.

Serve over steamed rice.

This will one day appear in yet another *Sweet Potato Queens®* book, God willing.

Equal Opportunity Soup*

6 large potatoes, peeled & cubed

½ cup shredded carrots

6 cups chicken broth, divided

1½ cups celery, chopped

1 cup onion, chopped fine

2 TBSP olive oil

1 cup heavy cream

½ cup milk

2 TBSP sour cream

2 TBSP salted butter

1 TBSP white wine Worcestershire sauce

2½ TBSP lemon juice

Hot pepper sauce to taste

Salt and pepper to taste

In an 8-qt. heavy pot, cook potatoes and carrots in 4 cups chicken broth until tender. Remove half from pot, mash and return to pot. In a skillet, cook celery and onion in oil until tender then add to potato pot. Stir in remaining broth, cream, milk, butter, sour cream, Worcestershire sauce, lemon juice, pepper sauce, salt, and pepper. Cook, stirring, over *LOW* heat for 15 mins. Good hot or cold.

*No sweet potatoes are used in this dish.

This will one day appear in yet another *Sweet Potato Queens® book*, God willing

GEORGE'S WHITE CHILI

4 TBSP olive oil, divided

8 boneless, skinless chicken breasts, cubed

1 large onion, chopped

5 ribs celery, chopped

2 TBSP roasted chopped garlic

3 cans chicken broth

3 cans white beans, with liquid
(15.5 oz. cans Great Northern or Navy)

2 cans white beans, with liquid, MASHED

2 4.5-oz. cans chopped green chilis

½ tsp. celery salt

1 tsp. oregano

1 tsp. cumin

½ tsp. chili powder

½ tsp. white pepper

½ tsp. cayenne pepper

1 tsp. salt

In an 8-qt. heavy pot, heat 2 TBSP olive oil then lightly brown chicken. Add remaining olive oil, onion, celery, and garlic — cook until onions are translucent.

(Continues on the next page.)

Add chicken broth, beans (whole and mashed), chilis, and all seasonings. Bring to a *Boil* then cover and reduce heat to *Simmer* 20-30 mins., stirring occasionally to prevent sticking. If the consistency is not of desired thickness, make a Slurry and add as necessary.

Slurry

2−4 TBSP corn starch

Water

Create a Slurry in a cup or small a bowl by combining corn starch with just enough cold water to dissolve it. (Make a small amount of Slurry to start.) Put the Slurry into the heated broth and stir constantly until it thickens to the desired consistency. Make more Slurry if necessary.

Serve over rice, topped with sour cream and shredded Mozzarella cheese. Freezes well.

(Revised/improved from original version.)

The Sweet Potato Queens' Big-Ass Cookbook (and Financial Planner)
(Three Rivers Press, 2003), p. 211

Nana's Sacred Matzo Ball Soup

1 whole chicken, cut up

1 gal. water

3 cloves garlic

2 tsp. salt

1 large onion, peeled & quartered

4 or 5 large carrots, cut in 1-inch pieces

2 stalks celery, cut in 1-inch pieces

Parsley

Dill

In a large, heavy pot, cook all together until chicken is done. Remove chicken, shred meat, discarding bones, fat, and skin. Strain broth and taste for "chickeny" strength—if it seems weak, add chicken bouillon to taste. Put chicken back in broth and keep *Simmering* till Matzo Balls are ready.

(Continues on the next page.)

Matzo Balls

½ cup Manischewitz® Matzo Meal *(No substitutes!)*

2 large eggs, beaten

1 tsp. salt

2 TBSP chicken fat

2 TBSP chicken broth

1½ quarts water

Mix Manischewitz® Matzo Meal, eggs, salt, fat, and broth. Cover and refrigerate (about 20 mins.) until it is a consistency that is easy to shape into 1-inch balls. Bring water to *Brisk Boil*. Reduce heat to *LOW* and drop balls in, being careful not to "crowd" the pot. Cover pot and *Boil* for 40 to 60 mins. Test for softness before removing—should be soft all through. Add water and cook longer if necessary. When soft, remove from water and place directly into the Chicken Soup to absorb flavor. Cook in soup on *LOW* for 15-20 mins.

*This should make about five (5) Matzo Balls.

It is recommended to have 4 pots of water boiling simultaneously, mixing up entire box of meal, making many balls at once and freezing for future soup.

The Sweet Potato Queens' Field Guide to Men:
Every Man I Love is Either Married, Gay, or Dead
(Three Rivers Press, 2004), p. 223

SOPA DE QUESO PARA MI AMADO PASTOR
(AKA Cheese Soup for my Beloved Pastor)

½ cup salted butter

1 cup chopped onion

1 cup grated carrot

1 cup celery, chopped fine

½ cup flour

8 cups heavy cream

8 cups chicken broth

¼ tsp. baking soda

6 jars Kraft® Old English Cheese or 8 cups shredded cheese
(Sharp Cheddar or Cheddar with habaneros)

Paprika or cayenne

In an 8-qt. heavy pot, cook vegetables in butter until very tender. Stir in flour, mix well. Add cream, chicken broth, baking soda and cheese. Cook, stirring, over *LOW* heat until cheese is melted. Serve sprinkled with either paprika or cayenne.

This will one day appear in yet another *Sweet Potato Queens®* book, God willing.

SOPA SABROSA
(AKA Yummy Soup)

3 lbs. boneless, skinless, chicken thighs

1 28 oz. can green enchilada sauce

24 ozs. chicken broth

2 cups Monterey Jack or Pepper Jack cheese, shredded

8 ozs. whipped cream cheese

4 ozs. salsa verde (8 ozs., if spicier is preferred)

1 cup heavy cream

1 bag (10-12 ozs.) frozen cut leaf spinach (may use fresh)

If thawed chicken is used, first cut it into bite-size pieces then along with enchilada sauce and chicken broth, put it all into a Crock-Pot® and cook on *LOW/MEDIUM* for around 6 hours. (If chicken is frozen before cooking, cut into bite-size pieces after cooking.) Stir in cheese and cream cheese until melted then add salsa and spinach. Slowly stir in cream.

This will one day appear in yet another *Sweet Potato Queens® book*, God willing.

TREVOR'S FAMOUS F & M PATIO BAR® JAMBALAYA

2 lbs. Andouille or smoked sausage

1 lb. ham (not processed)

1 lb. cut up chicken meat

5 onions, chopped

4 ribs celery, chopped

2 bell peppers, chopped

1 12-oz. beer

1 20-oz. can whole tomatoes

7 cups chicken stock

5 bay leaves

1 TBSP basil

1 TBSP thyme

1 TBSP chili powder

Salt

Pepper

4 cups rice (NOT converted)

In a large, heavy pot, brown sausage and ham, then add chicken and cook until just done. Add onions, celery, peppers, and beer. Stir frequently to prevent sticking. Cook until onions are clear, then break up the tomatoes with your hands and add them. Cook for 10 mins. then add stock, bay leaves, basil, thyme, chili

(Continues on the next page.)

powder, salt, and pepper—*Simmer* for 20 mins. Add rice and bring to *High Boil* for 4 mins.—then cover and reduce heat to LOWEST POSSIBLE SETTING. Cook, COVERED, for 20 mins. then check the rice for doneness. Turn all gently from bottom to top—if rice needs more time, cover then cook for another 10 mins. Salt and pepper to taste.

The Sweet Potato Queens' Big-Ass Cookbook (and Financial Planner)
(Three Rivers Press, 2003), p. 91

YUMMY SOUP
(AKA Sopa Sabrosa)

3 lbs. boneless, skinless, chicken thighs

1 28 oz. can green enchilada sauce

24 ozs. chicken broth

2 cups Monterey Jack or Pepper Jack cheese, shredded

8 ozs. whipped cream cheese

4 ozs. salsa verde (8 ozs., if spicier is preferred)

1 cup heavy cream

1 bag (10-12 ozs.) frozen cut leaf spinach (may use fresh)

If thawed chicken is used, first cut it into bite-size pieces then along with enchilada sauce and chicken broth, put it all into a Crock-Pot® and cook on *LOW/MEDIUM* for around 6 hours. (If chicken is frozen before cooking, cut into bite-size pieces after cooking.) Stir in cheese and cream cheese until melted then add salsa and spinach. Slowly stir in cream.

This will one day appear in yet another *Sweet Potato Queens® book*, God willing.

SWEETS

(Continues on the next page.)

(Continues on the next page.)

(Continues on the next page.)

A LITTLE SOMETHING FROM LITTLE JEFFREY

4 sticks salted butter

1 16-oz. box dark brown sugar

1 12-oz. bag semi-sweet chocolate chips

NOTE:
A candy thermometer is a must!

In a LARGE (4-qt.) sauce pan, with candy thermometer in pan, melt butter with brown sugar. Cook, stirring constantly, until it reaches 270°F. Remove from heat and pour onto cookie sheet, spreading with spatula to desired thickness. Cool for one minute, then pour chocolate chips over toffee as evenly as possible, spreading with spatula as chips melt. Refrigerate until hard, then break into pieces to serve.

KEEP IN MIND: Use a bigger pan than you think you need; it seems to "grow" as it heats. Do not let the thermometer touch the side or bottom of the pan or you will get a false reading. When it is almost ready, it will start to smell as if it is burning—this is normal. If you cook it for a shorter time, the toffee will be softer, cook it longer and it will be harder—suit yourself. Just don't burn it.

This may be my favorite recipe for the next _Sweet Potato Queens®_ book.

ACTUAL APPLE CAKE

3 cups apples, peeled & chopped

1-1/3 cups oil

2 cups sugar

2 large eggs

2½ cups flour

1 tsp. baking soda

1 tsp. salt

1 tsp. baking powder

1 running over tsp. vanilla

1 cup pecans, chopped

Whipped cream, optional

Preheat oven to 350°F. Mix together oil, sugar and eggs. Sift together flour, soda, salt, and baking powder. Gradually combine dry and creamy mixtures, then add vanilla. Gently fold in apples and pecans. Put into a greased 13″ x 9″ x 2″ pan and bake for approx. one hour. Cool, top with whipped cream, if desired, then serve.

The Sweet Potato Queens' Big-Ass Cookbook (and Financial Planner)
(Three Rivers Press, 2003), p. 30

APPLE CRACK
(AKA Yes, It's One More Dump Cake Variation)

2 20-oz. cans apple pie filling

2 sticks salted butter, melted

1 box yellow cake mix

1 cup dark brown sugar

1 tsp. cinnamon

2 cups pecan pieces

Preheat oven to 350°F. Spread pie filling into a 13" x 9" x 2" pan, sprayed with Pam®. Mix together melted butter, cake mix, brown sugar, cinnamon, and pecans. Spread evenly over pie filling. Bake for 40-45 mins. until brown and crispy on top. (Watch pecans for over-browning, cover pan loosely with foil if necessary.)

The Sweet Potato Queens' Guide to Raising Children for Fun and Profit
(Simon & Schuster, 2008), p. 86

ATLANTA ALLELUJAH!

1 chocolate cake mix

1 egg

1 stick salted butter, melted

<u>Topping</u>

1 8-oz. pkg. cream cheese, softened

2 eggs

1 running over tsp. vanilla

1 stick salted butter, melted

¾ cup peanut butter

1 16-oz. box powdered sugar

Preheat oven to 350°F. Mix cake mix, egg, and butter. Pour into a greased 13" x 9" x 2" pan. TOPPING: Stir together cream cheese, eggs, vanilla, butter, and peanut butter. Then add powdered sugar and mix well. Spread over cake mixture and bake for 40-50 mins.

Don't overcook—should be slightly gooey in center.

The Sweet Potato Queens' Big-Ass Cookbook (and Financial Planner)
(Three Rivers Press, 2003), p. 112

BETTER THAN SEX WITH THAT EX CAKE

1 German Chocolate cake mix,
prepared according to directions
¾ cup hot fudge sauce
¾ cup caramel sauce
¾ cup Eagle Brand® Sweetened Condensed Milk
6 large Heath® bars, crumbled, divided
Extra Creamy CoolWhip®

After cake is cooled, punch holes in it with the handle of a wooden spoon. Pour the fudge sauce over it and allow to sink in, then repeat with caramel sauce, followed by condensed milk. Sprinkle half of the Heath® bar crumbles over the top then cover with CoolWhip® and sprinkle the remaining Heath® bar crumbles on that.

The Sweet Potato Queens' Wedding Planner and Divorce Guide
(Crown Publishers, 2007), *Divorce Guide* side, p. 107

BEULAH LAND BOO-BOO PIE

Topping

1 14-oz. can Eagle Brand® Sweetened Condensed Milk

1 7-oz. pkg. coconut

Pie

½ cup salted butter

3 oz. (squares) unsweetened chocolate

¾ cup sugar

½ cup flour

3 eggs

1 running over tsp. vanilla

Preheat oven to 325°F. Mix together coconut and condensed milk and set aside. In a sauce pan, melt together butter and chocolate. Stir in sugar, flour, eggs and vanilla. Pour into a greased 9" pie pan. Spread coconut mixture over the top. Leave ½ inch border UNCOVERED by topping because, as it bakes, the bottom layer comes up and makes its own "crust." Bake for about 25 mins.

The Sweet Potato Queens' First Big-Ass Novel:
Stuff we didn't actually do, but could have, and may yet
(Simon & Schuster, 2008), p. 289

BIRTHDAY CAKE FOR A TRUE FRIEND ONLY

1½ cups salted butter, softened

2 cups dark brown sugar, packed

1 cup sugar

5 large eggs

3 cups flour

1 tsp. baking powder

½ tsp. salt

½ cup heavy cream

½ cup milk

1 8-oz. bag toffee-brickle bits

1 cup pecans, chopped

Preheat oven to 325°F. Beat together butter and sugars; add eggs one at a time. Separately, combine flour, baking powder, and salt. Add flour mix to sugar mixture slowly, alternating with cream/milk. Beat just until well blended. Stir in brickle and pecans. Put into a greased 12-cup Bundt pan and bake for 75-80 mins.—or until a toothpick comes out clean. (Cover cake loosely with foil to prevent burning top.)

(Continues on the next page.)

Cool in pan for 10 mins. then remove and cool on wire rack. When completely cool, make two layers by cutting cake in half horizontally with bread knife and poke holes in layers with a wooden spoon handle.

Icing

1 14-oz. can sweetened, condensed milk

1 cup dark brown sugar

2 TBSP salted butter

½ running over tsp. vanilla

Dash salt

In a sauce pan, combine condensed milk and brown sugar. Bring to a *Boil* over *MEDIUM-HIGH* heat, stirring frequently. Reduce heat and *Simmer*, stirring constantly for 3-5 mins. Remove from heat and stir in butter and vanilla. Cool for 5 mins., then pour over bottom layer of cake. Put top layer on and pour on remaining icing. If icing is overcooked, it will harden somewhat but it will still taste good.

This will one day appear in yet another *Sweet Potato Queens® book*, God willing.

BRIGADEIRAS

1 14-oz. can Eagle Brand® Sweetened Condensed Milk

3 TBSP Hershey's® cocoa

2 TBSP salted butter

Powdered sugar (optional)

Chocolate sprinkles (optional)

Chopped pecans (optional)

In a heavy sauce pan, mix together condensed milk and cocoa. Heat, stirring constantly, over *MEDIUM* heat. Will begin to thicken after about 10 mins. of *Gentle Boiling* — turn off heat and add butter. Stir well then allow to cool. While still warm, dampen palms and shape chocolate into little balls. May roll in powdered sugar, chocolate sprinkles, or chopped pecans or just eat plain.

The Sweet Potato Queens' Big-Ass Cookbook (and Financial Planner)
(Three Rivers Press, 2003), p. 160

BUTTERFINGER® CAKE

Cake

1 "butter recipe" yellow cake mix
1 running-over tsp. vanilla

Filling

1 8-oz. pkg. cream cheese
1 14-oz. can Eagle Brand® Sweetened Condensed Milk
1 8-oz tub Cool Whip®

Topping

20 ozs. Butterfinger® candy bars, chopped

Bake cake according to package directions, adding 1 running-over tsp. vanilla. Allow cake to cool completely.

Combine softened cream cheese, condensed milk, and CoolWhip® in food processor or with an electric handheld mixer.

(Continues on the next page.)

Options for Topping and Serving

Bake cake in two (2) 8″ layer pans, cover top of one with filling then top with chopped candy bars. Add second layer and repeat.

Or...

Bake cake in one (1) large, high-sided pan, cover top with filling and chopped candy bars.

The Sweet Potato Queens' Field Guide to Men:
Every Man I Love is Either Married, Gay, or Dead
(Three Rivers Press, 2004), p. 230

CARAMEL-Y COOKIES
(AKA HRH Jill's Favorite Cookie)

1 cup sugar

2 cups dark brown sugar

2 sticks salted butter

2 eggs

1 running-over teaspoon vanilla

2 cups flour

1 tsp. baking soda

1 tsp. salt

2 cups crushed corn flakes

¾ cup 1-minute oatmeal

¾ cup sweetened coconut, shredded

1 cup chopped pecans

Preheat oven to 350°F. In a mixing bowl, cream together sugars and butter, then add eggs and vanilla. Stir in flour, soda, and salt. Add corn flakes, oatmeal, coconut, and pecans. Mix well—use hands, if necessary, to thoroughly combine all ingredients. Drop by teaspoonful on a cookie sheet, lined with parchment paper or non-stick foil. Bake for 11½ minutes, 12 minutes if you like them crispier.

This will one day appear in yet another *Sweet Potato Queens® book*, God willing.

Catshit Cookies

1 stick salted butter

½ cup Hershey's® cocoa

2 cups sugar

½ cup milk

3 cups quick oats (*never* Instant)

½ cup peanut butter

1 running-over tsp. vanilla

Melt together butter, cocoa, sugar and milk in pan, cooking just until bubbles form around the sides. Remove from heat and add oats, peanut butter, and vanilla. Mix well and drop by spoonfuls onto wax paper. Allow to cool before serving.

The Sweet Potato Queens' Big-Ass Cookbook (and Financial Planner)
(Three Rivers Press, 2003), p. 45

CHOCOLATE GRAVY AND BISCUITS

3 TBSP flour

2 TBSP Hershey's® cocoa

Dash salt

4 TBSP sugar

2 cups milk

2 TBSP salted butter

1 running-over tsp. vanilla

1 can refrigerated biscuits,

baked according to package

Combine flour, cocoa, salt, and sugar in pot. Stir in milk and cook over *MEDIUM-HIGH* heat until it bubbles and thickens then add butter and vanilla. Stir until butter is melted and well-blended. Split cooked biscuits and pour gravy over them to serve.

The Sweet Potato Queens' Big-Ass Cookbook (and Financial Planner)
(Three Rivers Press, 2003), p. 43

CHOCOLATE STUFF
(This is my personal all-time, favorite recipe.)

2 eggs

1 cup sugar

½ cup flour

¼ tsp. salt

1 stick salted butter

2 TBSP Hershey's® cocoa

1 running over tsp. vanilla

1 cup pecan pieces, optional

Preheat oven to 300°F. Beat eggs and stir in sugar, then flour. Melt together butter and cocoa then add to egg mixture. Add vanilla, and pecans, if desired. Pour into a greased loaf pan then put loaf pan into a larger pan filled with water. Bake for 40 to 50 mins.

*NOTE: Many ovens lose calibration below 350°F. This SHOULD end up being slightly crunchy on top, gooey on bottom. If it never hardens on top, your oven is probably too cool. It will still taste great—just serve it over ice cream and up the temp on your oven the next time you make it.

The Sweet Potato Queens Book of Love
(Three Rivers Press, 1999), p. 169

and

The Sweet Potato Queens' Big-Ass Cookbook (and Financial Planner)
(Three Rivers Press, 2003), p. 255

CHOCOLATOPOLOUS
(AKA I've Felt Better but It Took Longer and Cost More)

2 cups sugar

2 cups flour

½ cup salted butter

½ cup shortening

3 TBSP Hershey's® cocoa

1 cup Coca-Cola®

½ cup buttermilk

1 tsp. baking soda

2 eggs, beaten

¼ tsp. salt

1 running over tsp. vanilla

1-2 cups mini marshmallows

Preheat oven to 350°F. Combine sugar and flour. Melt together butter, shortening, cocoa, and Coke®. Pour into sugar/flour mixture. Add buttermilk, soda, eggs, salt, vanilla, and marshmallows. Pour into a greased 13" x 9" x 2" pan and be sure marshmallows are evenly distributed. Bake until top is "set." (About 40 mins., depending on oven but watch marshmallows for scorching. Cover pan loosely with foil if necessary.)

(Continues on the next page.)

Icing

3 TBSP Hershey's® cocoa

1 stick salted butter

6 TBSP Coca-Cola®

¼ tsp. salt

1 box powdered sugar

1 running over tsp. vanilla

Melt together butter, cocoa, Coke®, and salt. Stir in powdered sugar and add vanilla. Poke holes in cake to allow for icing to seep down. Pour hot icing over hot cake.

The Sweet Potato Queens' Big-Ass Cookbook (and Financial Planner)
(Three Rivers Press, 2003), p. 242

and

The Sweet Potato Queens' Wedding Planner and Divorce Guide
(Crown Publishers, 2007), *Divorce Guide* side, p. 104

COCONUT CARAMEL PIE*
(AKA Oh, GOD! Pie)

Crust

1½ cups flour

1 stick salted butter, softened

1 cup finely chopped pecans

Filling

1 8-oz. pkg. cream cheese, softened

1 14-oz. can Eagle Brand® Sweetened Condensed Milk

16 ozs. CoolWhip

Topping

1 7-oz. pkg. sweetened coconut flakes

½ stick salted butter, melted

1 cup pecan pieces

1 12-oz. jar caramel sauce

(Continues on the next page.)

Preheat oven to 350°F. In a mixing bowl, combine flour, butter, and pecans to make two (2) pie crusts. Mash into 9" pie pans and bake for 10 mins., until lightly browned. In a large bowl, mix together cream cheese, condensed milk, and CoolWhip®. Put into cooled pie crusts.

In a small bowl, combine coconut, butter, and pecan pieces. Spread evenly onto cookie sheet and toast it, stirring often to prevent burning. Put cooled toasted coconut mixture on top of pies and pour caramel sauce over the tops. Chill in freezer until set.

*In many early editions of the printed books, this pie is described as CHOCOLATE caramel pie—and there is obviously NO chocolate in it. It was a typo! It is CARAMEL coconut pie. To this very day, I still get emails from Queens, asking, "Where's the Chocolate?" Sigh.

The Sweet Potato Queens Book of Love
(Three Rivers Press, 1999), p. 175

and

The Sweet Potato Queens' Big-Ass Cookbook (and Financial Planner)
(Three Rivers Press, 2003), p. 257

COSMIC CLIMAX COOKIE CAKE

1 12-oz. box NILLA® wafers, crushed

1 cup salted butter

2 cups sugar

6 eggs

½ cup milk

1 7-oz. pkg. Coconut

1 cup chopped pecans

Preheat oven to 275°F. In a mixing bowl, cream together butter, sugar, and eggs. Slowly alternate adding NILLA® crumbs and milk. Then add coconut and pecans. Put into a greased, floured Bundt pan and bake for 1½ hours.

The Sweet Potato Queens' First Big-Ass Novel:
Stuff we didn't actually do, but could have, and may yet
(Simon & Schuster, 2008), p. 289

DANGER PUDDING & SAFE VERSION

1 14 oz. can Eagle Brand® Sweetened Condensed Milk, unopened

1 pot of water

Even though it plainly says on the label, "DO NOT HEAT UNOPENED CAN," we have repeatedly chosen to ignore it—feeling that the risk was well-worth it. We acknowledge that we have willfully put unopened cans into pots of water and boiled them for an hour or so until the sugar caramelized and created pudding.

DO NOT DO THAT!

Here's How to do it Safely:

1 14 oz. can Eagle Brand® Sweetened Condensed Milk

1 16-oz. canning jar

Water

Pour the milk into the canning jar then make sure the lid is screwed on TIGHT. Put the jar in a Crock-Pot® and cover completely with water. Turn Crock-Pot® on _HIGH_ for 4-6 hours, depending on desired consistency.

Original recipe:

The Sweet Potato Queens Book of Love
(Three Rivers Press, 1999), p. 178

ONLY use the above Safe Version _from now on!_

DELICIOUS DEATH DUMP CAKE

1 Butter Pecan cake mix

2 15-oz. cans crushed pineapple, juice included

1 stick salted butter, melted or cut into pats

Preheat oven to 350°F. Dump pineapple into a 2-qt. baking dish. Dump cake mix on top of that. Pour or put butter pats on top of that. Bake for about 30 mins. or until lightly browned.

The Sweet Potato Queens' First Big-Ass Novel:
Stuff we didn't actually do, but could have, and may yet
(Simon & Schuster, 2008), p. 290

DING DONGS® CAKE

1 large box instant chocolate pudding mix

1 box (10 ct.) chocolate Ding Dongs®, crumbled

1 8-oz. container CoolWhip®

1 Hershey® bar, grated

½ cup pecans, chopped

Make pudding according to package directions. Put half of the Ding Dongs® crumbles into a serving dish. Top with half of the pudding. Then repeat. Top with CoolWhip®, Hershey® bar shavings, and pecans.

The Sweet Potato Queens' Wedding Planner and Divorce Guide
(Crown Publishers, 2007), *Divorce Guide* side, p. 83

DINKSEY'S GOOEY BARS

1 Duncan Hines® devil's food cake mix

1 stick salted butter, melted

3 eggs

1 8-oz. pkg. cream cheese, softened

1 box powdered sugar

1 running over tsp. vanilla

1 cup chopped pecans

Preheat oven to 350°F. Mix together cake mix, butter, and 1 egg. Press into a greased 13" x 9" x 2" pan. In a mixing bowl, combine cream cheese, sugar, 2 eggs, vanilla, and pecans. Pour over cake mixture and bake for around 40 mins.

God Save the Sweet Potato Queens
(Three Rivers Press, 2001), p. 222

and

The Sweet Potato Queens' Big-Ass Cookbook (and Financial Planner)
(Three Rivers Press, 2003), p. 262

DON'T EVEN TASTE THESE IF
YOU DON'T PLAN TO EAT THEM ALL

1¼ cups salted butter, softened

2 cups sugar

2 eggs

2 running over tsp. vanilla

2 cups flour

¾ cup Hershey's® cocoa

1 tsp. baking soda

½ tsp. salt

Preheat oven to 350°F. In a mixing bowl, combine all ingredients and drop by spoonful onto a cookie sheet. Bake for 8-9 mins.

The Sweet Potato Queens' Wedding Planner and Divorce Guide
(Crown Publishers, 2007), *Divorce Guide* side, p. 105

Drop-Dead-Easy Pots de Crème

¾ cup heavy cream

1 egg

6 ozs. semi-sweet chocolate chips

1/8 tsp. salt

2 TBSP sugar

1 TBSP bourbon or brandy

Heat cream just to *Boiling Point*. In blender or food processor, put egg, chocolate chips, salt, and sugar. Blend on *HIGH* for about 20 seconds. With processor running, slowly pour the hot cream in. Turn off and add liquor, then blend for another few seconds. Pour into small ramekins or demitasse cups and chill before serving.

The Sweet Potato Queens' Big-Ass Cookbook (and Financial Planner)
(Three Rivers Press, 2003), p. 111

FUZZY NAVEL CAKE

½ cup dark brown sugar

1 29-oz. can peach slices, well-drained

Maraschino cherries

1 yellow cake mix

1 3.5-oz. pkg. vanilla instant pudding

¾ cup orange juice

½ cup oil

¼ cup peach schnapps

1 TBSP grated orange peel

4 eggs

Topping

2 TBSP salted butter, melted

2 TBSP peach schnapps

1/8 tsp. cinnamon

(Continues on the next page.)

Whipped Cream

1 cup heavy whipping cream

1 TBSP powdered sugar

2 TBSP peach schnapps

Preheat oven to 350°F. Grease and flour 12-cup Bundt pan. Sprinkle brown sugar evenly on bottom and arrange peach slices on top of sugar, putting a cherry between the peach slices. In a large bowl, combine cake mix, pudding mix, juice, oil, schnapps, orange peel, and eggs. Beat on *HIGH* mixer speed for 2 mins. then pour over sugar/peaches in Bundt pan and bake at 55-60 mins. Watch for over-browning, cover loosely with foil if necessary to prevent. Cool for 15 mins. then poke deep holes in cake with a bamboo skewer. Mix together melted butter, schnapps, and cinnamon. Pour over warm cake. Using an electric handheld mixer, whip cream to soft peaks then add sugar and schnapps and whip again briefly. Top each piece of warm cake with a dollop.

The Sweet Potato Queens' Wedding Planner and Divorce Guide
(Crown Publishers, 2007), *Divorce Guide* side, p. 120

"Get Back, Granny" Sweet Potato Cobbler

Filling

2-3 cups sweet potatoes (canned or fresh cooked),
cut into small chunks
1 stick salted butter
2 cups water
2 cups sugar

Dough

1½ cups self-rising flour
½ cup shortening
1/3 cup milk
1 tsp. cinnamon
1 tsp. nutmeg

Preheat oven to 350°F. Melt butter in 13" x 9" x 2" pan and set aside. Heat water and sugar together until sugar is completely melted. Make dough and turn out onto a well-floured surface; roll out to rectangle about ¼" thick. Sprinkle dough with cinnamon and nutmeg. Spread sweet potatoes over dough, roll it up then pinch ends together to seal. Slice the roll into 15 or 20 pieces and put them in the melted butter. Pour the sugar mixture over it all and bake for about 45 mins.

God Save the Sweet Potato Queens
(Three Rivers Press, 2001), p. 220

GOOIEST CAKE IN THE WORLD

1 yellow cake mix (not pudding kind)

3 eggs

¼ cup water

1 tsp. baking soda

¼ tsp. salt

1 20-oz. can crushed pineapple

Preheat oven to 350°F. In a mixing bowl, combine cake mix, eggs, water, soda, salt, and pineapple. Bake in greased cake pans until toothpick put in center comes out clean.

Icing

2 sticks salted butter

1 cup evaporated milk

1½ cups sugar

7 ozs. Baker's Angel Flake® Coconut

In a sauce pan, melt together butter, evaporated milk and sugar. Add coconut. Poke holes in cake layers with a wooden spoon handle and pour hot icing over them.

The Sweet Potato Queens' Big-Ass Cookbook (and Financial Planner)
(Three Rivers Press, 2003), p. 107

HEAVEN IS A PLACE CALLED HICKORY PIT
(AKA Hershey® Bar Pie)

Oreo® crust (pre-made or DIY below)

Salted butter

½ cup milk

16 large marshmallows

6 Hershey® bars with almonds

Additional almonds, as desired

1 cup whipping cream, whipped OR

1 8-oz. tub CoolWhip®

DIY Oreo® crust: With a kitchen mallet crush Oreos® in a Ziploc-type bag; in a mixing bowl combine mashed Oreo® crumbs with enough melted butter to hold it together then press Oreos® into a 9" pie pan.

Heat milk and marshmallows in double boiler until melted. Add candy bars and stir until melted together. Add more almonds, if you like. Cool. Stir in either whipped cream or CoolWhip®, pour into crust and chill overnight. Top with additional whipped cream or CoolWhip® and a sprinkling of Oreo® crumbs before serving.

The Sweet Potato Queens' First Big-Ass Novel:
Stuff we didn't actually do, but could have, and may yet
(Simon & Schuster, 2008), p. 290

and

The Sweet Potato Queens' Big-Ass Cookbook (and Financial Planner)
(Three Rivers Press, 2003), p. 215

HERSHEY® BAR PIE
(AKA Heaven is a Place Called Hickory Pit)

Oreo® crust (pre-made or DIY below)

Salted butter

½ cup milk

16 large marshmallows

6 Hershey® bars with almonds

Additional almonds, as desired

1 cup whipping cream, whipped OR

1 8-oz. tub CoolWhip®

DIY Oreo® crust: With a kitchen mallet crush Oreos® in a Ziploc-type bag; in a mixing bowl combine mashed Oreo® crumbs with enough melted butter to hold it together then press Oreos® into a 9″ pie pan.

Heat milk and marshmallows in double boiler until melted. Add candy bars and stir until melted together. Add more almonds, if you like. Cool. Stir in either whipped cream or CoolWhip®, pour into crust and chill overnight. Top with additional whipped cream or CoolWhip® and a sprinkling of Oreo® crumbs before serving.

The Sweet Potato Queens' First Big-Ass Novel:
Stuff we didn't actually do, but could have, and may yet
(Simon & Schuster, 2008), p. 290

and

The Sweet Potato Queens' Big-Ass Cookbook (and Financial Planner)
(Three Rivers Press, 2003), p. 215

HOLLY SPRINGS HILL COUNTRY HAPPYCAKES

Graham crackers

1½ sticks salted butter

1 cup sugar

1 egg

½ cup milk

1 cup chopped pecans

1 cup Graham cracker crumbs

1 cup shredded coconut

Line a 13" x 9" x 2" pan with whole Graham crackers. In a sauce pan, melt butter and add sugar, stirring until smooth. Combine egg and milk and stir into butter mixture, bringing to *Boil*, stirring constantly. Remove from heat and add pecans, crumbs, and coconut. Pour over Graham crackers in the flat pan. Add another layer of whole Graham crackers.

(Continues on the next page.)

Topping

2 cups powdered sugar

1 running over tsp. vanilla

½ stick salted butter, melted

3 TBSP milk

Topping: In a mixing bowl, blend together sugar, vanilla, melted butter, and milk. Pour over top of crackers and chill. Cut into squares when set. Best served at room temperature.

Fat Is The New 30:
The Sweet Potato Queens' Guide to Coping with (the crappy parts of) Life
(Amazon Publishing, 2012), p. 142

HRH JILL'S FAVORITE COOKIE
(AKA Caramel-y Cookies)

1 cup sugar

2 cups dark brown sugar

2 sticks salted butter

2 eggs

1 running-over teaspoon vanilla

2 cups flour

1 tsp. baking soda

1 tsp. salt

2 cups crushed corn flakes

¾ cup 1-minute oatmeal

¾ cup sweetened coconut, shredded

1 cup chopped pecans

Preheat oven to 325°F. In a mixing bowl, cream together sugars and butter, then add eggs and vanilla. Stir in flour, soda, and salt. Add corn flakes, oatmeal, coconut, and pecans. Mix well—use hands, if necessary, to thoroughly combine all ingredients. Drop by teaspoonful on a cookie sheet, lined with parchment paper or non-stick foil. Bake for 11½ minutes, 12 minutes if you like them crispier.

This will one day appear in yet another *Sweet Potato Queens®* book, God willing.

I-Can't-See-My-Feet-But-Who-Cares Krispy Kreme® Bread Puddin'
(AKA Krispy Kreme® Bread Puddin')

1 dozen regular glazed Krispy Kreme® doughnuts

2 eggs, beaten

1 cup milk

2/3 cup Eagle Brand® Sweetened Condensed Milk

¼ tsp. salt

¼ tsp. cinnamon

½ running over tsp. vanilla

Preheat oven to 350°F. In large bowl, tear up the doughnuts. Mix together eggs, milk, and condensed milk then pour over doughnut pieces. Add salt, cinnamon, and vanilla. Stir up gently and put into greased loaf pans and bake for 40 mins.

Icing

½ stick salted butter, melted

1¾ cup confectioner's sugar

2 TBSP brandy, rum (or any liquid desired; even milk works)

In a sauce pan, mix butter, sugar, and brandy. Pour over hot pudding as soon as its removed from the oven. Serve warm.

Fat Is The New 30:
The Sweet Potato Queens' Guide to Coping with (the crappy parts of) Life
(Amazon Publishing, 2012), p. 144

ITALIAN CREAM CAKE

5 eggs, separated

1 stick salted butter

½ cup shortening

2 cups sugar

2 cups cake flour

1 tsp. baking soda

½ tsp. salt

1 cup buttermilk

1 cup chopped pecans

7 ozs. Baker's Angel Flake® coconut

Preheat oven to 325°F. With an electric handheld mixer, beat egg whites into soft peaks. In a mixing bowl, cream together with mixer the butter, shortening, and sugar. Add egg yolks and beat well with mixer. Mix together flour, baking soda, and salt. Gradually stir in buttermilk and add all that to the egg yolk mixture. Stir in pecans and coconut. Then, gently fold in beaten egg whites. Put into three (3) greased and floured cake pans and bake until they test done at center.

(Continues on the next page.)

Icing

1 8-oz. pkg. cream cheese

1 stick salted butter

1 box confectioner's sugar

1 running over tsp. vanilla

Chopped pecans

In a bowl, beat together softened cream cheese and butter with sugar and vanilla. Apply to cake and top with chopped pecans.

The Sweet Potato Queens' Wedding Planner and Divorce Guide
(Crown Publishers, 2007), *Divorce Guide* side, p. 81

I'VE FELT BETTER BUT IT TOOK LONGER AND COST MORE
(AKA Chocolatopolous)

2 cups sugar

2 cups flour

½ cup salted butter

½ cup shortening

3 TBSP Hershey's® cocoa

1 cup Coca-Cola®

½ cup buttermilk

1 tsp. baking soda

2 eggs, beaten

¼ tsp. salt

1 running over tsp. vanilla

1-2 cups mini marshmallows

Preheat oven to 350°F. In a mixing bowl, combine sugar and flour. In a sauce pan, melt together butter, shortening, cocoa, and Coke®. Pour into sugar/flour mixture. Add buttermilk, soda, eggs, salt, vanilla, and marshmallows. Pour into a greased 13" x 9" x 2" pan. Make sure marshmallows are evenly distributed. Bake until top is "set." (About 40 mins., depending on oven but watch marshmallows for scorching. Cover pan loosely with foil if necessary.)

(Continues on the next page.)

Icing

3 TBSP Hershey's® cocoa

1 stick salted butter

6 TBSP Coca-Cola®

¼ tsp. salt

1 box powdered sugar

1 running over tsp. vanilla

In a sauce pan, melt together butter, cocoa, Coke®, and salt. Stir in powdered sugar and add vanilla. Poke holes in cake with a wooden spoon handle to allow for icing to seep down. Pour hot icing over hot cake.

The Sweet Potato Queens' Wedding Planner and Divorce Guide
(Crown Publishers, 2007), *Divorce Guide* side, p. 104

and

The Sweet Potato Queens' Big-Ass Cookbook (and Financial Planner)
(Three Rivers Press, 2003), p. 242

It's a Miracle! Pie

1 cup sugar

4 eggs

2 cups milk

½ cup salted butter, melted

½ cup flour

1 running over tsp. vanilla

1 cup flaked coconut

1/8 tsp. salt

Preheat oven to 300°F. Put all ingredients in food processor and blend well. Pour into a greased 9.5" pie pan and bake until it sets, about an hour. Makes its own crust.

The Sweet Potato Queens' Big-Ass Cookbook (and Financial Planner)
(Three Rivers Press, 2003), p. 113

JILL CONNER BROWNE-IES

1¼ sticks salted butter, melted

2 cups dark brown sugar

2 eggs, beaten

2 running over tsp. vanilla

1 cup flour

2 tsp. baking powder

¼ tsp. salt

Preheat oven to 350°F. In a bowl, mix all ingredients by hand and pour into a greased, appropriate-sized baking dish. Bake for 25-30 mins.

The Sweet Potato Queens' Wedding Planner and Divorce Guide
(Crown Publishers, 2007), *Divorce Guide* side, p. 106

Jim Frye's Sacred Dessert Recipe

5 TBSP salted butter

5 TBSP dark brown sugar

1 TBSP lemon juice

4 TBSP orange juice

2 cups sliced strawberries

Vanilla ice cream

2 TBSP Grand Marnier® Cordon Rouge (optional)

In large skillet, melt together butter and brown sugar, add juices and stir well. Add strawberries and cook over *LOW* heat, stirring, until berries soften to your preference. Serve over vanilla ice cream. (May top with Grand Marnier® and ignite with long match for brief flambé, if desired.)

The Sweet Potato Queens' Field Guide to Men:
Every Man I Love is Either Married, Gay, or Dead
(Three Rivers Press, 2004), p. 229

KRISPY KREME® BREAD PUDDIN'
(AKA I-Can't-See-My-Feet-But-Who-Cares Krispy Kreme® Bread Puddin')

1 dozen regular glazed Krispy Kreme® doughnuts

2 eggs, beaten

1 cup milk

2/3 cup Eagle Brand® Sweetened Condensed Milk

¼ tsp. salt

¼ tsp. cinnamon

½ running over tsp. vanilla

Preheat oven to 350°F. In large bowl, tear up the doughnuts. Mix together eggs, milk, and condensed milk then pour over doughnut pieces. Add salt, cinnamon, and vanilla. Stir up gently and put into greased loaf pans and bake for 40 mins.

Icing

½ stick salted butter, melted

1¾ cup confectioner's sugar

2 TBSP brandy, rum (or any liquid desired; even milk works)

In a sauce pan, mix butter, sugar, and brandy. Pour over hot pudding as soon as its removed from the oven. Serve warm.

Fat Is The New 30:
The Sweet Potato Queens' Guide to Coping with (the crappy parts of) Life
(Amazon Publishing, 2012), p. 144

LAZY, LOW-RENT, AND LUSCIOUS PECAN PUDDIN'

1 ready-made pecan pie
1 12-oz. tub CoolWhip®

In a bowl, smash pie into mush and mix thoroughly with CoolWhip®. Spoon into small ramekins or demitasse cups or into larger serving dishes.

Never admit to anyone how you made this!

The Sweet Potato Queens' Big-Ass Cookbook (and Financial Planner)
(Three Rivers Press, 2003), p. 174

LEMON YUMBO

Crust/Topping

1¼ cups *unsweetened* coconut

¾ cup Saltine cracker crumbs

½ cup sugar

½ cup flour

1 stick salted butter, softened

Preheat oven to 400°F. In a bowl, mix coconut, cracker crumbs, sugar, flour, and butter. Press half of it into a greased 8" x 8" pan.

Filling

½ cup sugar

2½ TBSP cornstarch

¼ tsp. salt

1-1/3 cups milk

1 egg, beaten

¼ tsp. lemon juice

½ tsp. grated lemon peel

1 TBSP salted butter

Few drops vanilla

(Continues on the next page.)

In a sauce pan, mix sugar, cornstarch, salt, and milk, then cook over *LOW* heat, stirring constantly, until thickened. Mix beaten egg with lemon juice then add a little of the hot milk mixture to it. Add the lemon/egg to the rest of the hot milk mixture, cook and stir over *LOW* heat for 2 mins. Remove from heat and stir in lemon peel, butter, and vanilla.

Pour Filling into coconut crust and put remaining half of crust/topping on top. Bake for 25 mins. or just until golden brown. Chill before serving.

The Sweet Potato Queens' Big-Ass Cookbook (and Financial Planner)
(Three Rivers Press, 2003), p. 106

Linda's Killer Cake with No Apples

1 yellow cake mix

4 eggs

¾ cup oil

1 cup water

1 can Betty Crocker® Rich and Creamy Coconut Pecan Frosting

Preheat oven to 350°F. In a bowl, combine cake mix with eggs, oil, and water. Stir in frosting. Transfer to a Bundt pan then bake for approx. one hour. Test for doneness with toothpick.

The Sweet Potato Queens' Big-Ass Cookbook (and Financial Planner)
(Three Rivers Press, 2003), p. 29

LORENE'S PRALINES

2 cups sugar

1 tsp. baking soda

1 cup buttermilk

1/8 tsp. salt

2 TBSP salted butter

2½ cups pecan pieces

In a heavy sauce pan, combine sugar, baking soda, buttermilk, and salt. Cook on *HIGH*, stirring constantly for 5 mins. Add butter and pecans and cook for a few more minutes over *MEDIUM* heat. Remove from heat and cool slightly then beat with a wooden spoon until thick and creamy. Drop by spoonfuls onto wax paper and allow to harden.

The Sweet Potato Queens' Big-Ass Cookbook (and Financial Planner)
(Three Rivers Press, 2003), p. 19

MARTHA JEAN'S BY-GAWD APPLE ENCHILADAS

6-8 flour tortillas

Apple pie filling

Cinnamon

½ cup salted butter

½ cup sugar

½ cup dark brown sugar

½ cup water

Preheat oven to 350°F. Put pie filling in tortillas, roll up and put them seam down in a baking pan and sprinkle with cinnamon. In a sauce pan, melt together butter, sugars, and water. Bring to a *Boil* and *Simmer* for about 3 mins. Pour over tortillas and let it sit for about 30 mins. Bake for 20 mins. Serve hot with vanilla ice cream.

American Thighs:
The Sweet Potato Queens' Guide to Preserving Your Assets
(Simon & Schuster, 2009), p. 296

Maw Maw's Shortbread
(Three Variations)

Version #1

1½ cups flour

½ tsp. salt

1 stick + 2½ TBSP salted butter, softened or melted

½ cup *LIGHT* brown sugar

Preheat to 325°F. In a mixing bowl, cream together sugar and butter. Add flour and salt, mixing well. Dough will be stiff. Spread evenly in a greased 8″ x 8″ baking dish. Bake for 30-35 mins. Cool completely before slicing to serve.

Version #2

2 cups flour

½ tsp. salt

2 sticks salted butter, softened or melted

3/4 cup *LIGHT* brown sugar

Preheat to 325°F. In a mixing bowl, cream together sugar and butter. Add flour and salt, mixing well. Dough will be stiff. Spread evenly in a greased 8″ x 8″ baking dish. Bake for 30-35 mins. Cool completely before slicing to serve.

(Version #3 on the next page.)

Version #3

2 cups ALL-purpose flour

½ tsp. salt

2 sticks salted butter, softened or melted

3/4 cup powdered sugar

Preheat to 325°F. In a mixing bowl, cream together sugar and butter. Add flour and salt, mixing well. Dough will be stiff. Spread evenly in a greased 8" x 8" baking dish. Bake for 30-35 mins. Cool completely before slicing to serve.

These will one day appear in yet another *Sweet Potato Queens®* *book,* God willing.

MIMI'S BUTTERFINGER® COOKIES

1 cup sugar

1-1/3 cups dark brown sugar

1 stick salted butter

4 eggs

3 running-over tsp. vanilla

2½ cups chunky peanut butter

2 cups flour

1 tsp. baking soda

½ tsp. salt

20 ozs. Butterfinger® bars, chopped

Preheat oven to 350°F. In a bowl, mix together—using an electric handheld mixer if you have one—sugars, butter, eggs, and vanilla. Add peanut butter and mix. Add flour, baking soda, and salt, stirring well, then add Butterfingers®. Drop by spoonfuls onto a lightly greased cookie sheet and bake for 10-11 mins.

The Sweet Potato Queens Book of Love
(Three Rivers Press, 1999), p. 179

and

The Sweet Potato Queens' Big-Ass Cookbook (and Financial Planner)
(Three Rivers Press, 2003), p. 258

Miss Lexie's Pineapple Casserole
(AKA Pineapple Stuff)

1 20-oz. can pineapple in juice, chunks or tidbits

3 TBSP juice

½ cup sugar

3 TBSP flour

1 cup Sharp Cheddar cheese, shredded

2 TBSP salted butter

½ cup Ritz® cracker crumbs

Preheat oven to 350°F. Drain pineapple and retain 3 TBSP juice. In a bowl, mix juice with sugar and flour. Stir mixture into pineapple with cheese. Put into a greased, appropriate-sized baking dish. In a sauce pan, melt butter then stir in cracker crumbs. Top pineapple with buttered crumbs then bake for 20-30 mins. Can be frozen.

The Sweet Potato Queens Book of Love
(Three Rivers Press, 1999), p. 182

and

The Sweet Potato Queens' Big-Ass Cookbook (and Financial Planner)
(Three Rivers Press, 2003), p. 258

MOTOR HOME MARVEL

12-18 ice cream sandwiches
(chocolate wafer, vanilla ice cream)
1 jar caramel sauce
CoolWhip®
Heath Bar® brickle, plain or chocolate

Cram the ice cream sandwiches into a pan. Poke holes in the wafers with a wooden spoon handle and pour the caramel sauce over the top. Spread CoolWhip® over that and sprinkle liberally with brickle. Put in freezer and keep frozen until serving.

The Sweet Potato Queens' Big-Ass Cookbook (and Financial Planner)
(Three Rivers Press, 2003), p. 173

MYSTERY MUSH

Regular Oreos® (at least 16)

8 ozs. chopped dates

½ tsp. salt

1 cup water

2 cups mini-marshmallows

1 running-over tsp. vanilla

½ cup pecans, halves (optional)

½ pint whipping cream

DIY Oreo® crust: With a kitchen mallet crush Oreos® in a Ziploc-type bag; in a mixing bowl combine mashed Oreo® crumbs with enough melted butter to hold it together then press Oreos® into a 9" pie pan.

In a sauce pan, bring to a *Boil* dates, salt, and water. Reduce heat and *Simmer* for 3 mins. Remove from heat and add marshmallows. Allow to cool. Add vanilla and pecans, mixing well. Pour into Oreo® crust. Using an electric handheld mixer, whip cream to soft peaks; spread over pie then top with Oreo® crumbs and pecan halves, if desired. Chill before serving.

The Sweet Potato Queens' Big-Ass Cookbook (and Financial Planner)
(Three Rivers Press, 2003), p. 107

New & Improved Peaches*

6 peaches, peeled, halved, & pitted

1 stick salted butter, melted

3-4 TBSP cinnamon/sugar**

4 ozs. cream cheese, softened

1 egg yolk

¼ cup sugar

1½ running over tsp. vanilla

Preheat oven to 350°F. Cut thin slice off the bottom of each peach half so it will sit flat in a greased 13" x 9" x 2" pan. Pour melted butter evenly over peaches and sprinkle with cinnamon/sugar. In a bowl, combine cream cheese, egg yolk, sugar, and vanilla. Put a spoonful in each peach. Bake for 30 mins.

*If Georgia peaches are NOT *in season*, do NOT bother with this recipe! You really cannot "improve" a peach that is out of season—there is zero hope for them. Make something else.

**Good ratio for cinnamon to sugar mixture…but suit your own personal taste: ¼ cup sugar to 1 TBSP cinnamon.

This will one day appear in yet another *Sweet Potato Queens*® *book*, God willing.

No-Pain, Plenty-Gain Coffee Cake

1 pkg. (24) Parker House rolls, FROZEN

1 small pkg. instant butterscotch pudding mix

1 cup dark brown sugar

2 TBSP cinnamon

1 stick salted butter, melted

½ cup pecan pieces

Preheat oven to 350°F. In a bowl, mix together pudding mix, brown sugar, cinnamon, butter, and pecans. Put half the frozen rolls into a greased Bundt pan. Top with half the pudding mixture. Put remaining rolls on top of that layer and then add the remaining pudding mixture. Cover loosely with foil sprayed with Pam®. Put a towel over it and let it sit on the counter overnight to rise. If the rolls rise over the top of the pan, just poke them down. Bake for 30 mins.

The Sweet Potato Queens' Big-Ass Cookbook (and Financial Planner)
(Three Rivers Press, 2003), p. 175

No-Spoons-Necessary Divinity*

2 ½ cups sugar

½ cup Karo® Light syrup (NOT "Lite")

½ cup water

¼ tsp. salt

2 egg whites, beaten

1 running over tsp. vanilla

Pecan halves

NOTE:
A candy thermometer is a must!

In a sauce pan, stir together sugar, Karo®, water and salt. Cook over *MEDIUM* heat, stirring constantly until sugar is dissolved and it reaches 260°F or "hard-ball" stage. Remove from heat immediately. Gradually pour a thin stream of the syrup mixture over the beaten egg whites, while continuing to beat with mixer. Add vanilla and beat on *HIGH* speed for 5 more mins. or until stiff peaks form. Drop by teaspoonfuls onto wax paper and top each with a pecan half. Allow to harden before serving.

*Preferably, it should be a cold, dry, and sunshiny day for making divinity.

The Sweet Potato Queens' Big-Ass Cookbook (and Financial Planner)
(Three Rivers Press, 2003), p. 15

NOT-SOUTHERN JUNIOR LEAGUE YUMMIES

1 cup salted butter

1 cup dark brown sugar

Saltine crackers

1 12-oz. bag chocolate chips

6 ozs. Heath Bar® brickle bits (*plain,* NOT chocolate)

Preheat oven to 350°F. Line a RIMMED cookie sheet with foil then grease the foil. Put a layer of Saltines on foil, covering whole pan, crackers touching. Put butter and brown sugar in small sauce pan and bring to *Boil, Simmer* for about 5 mins. Pour over crackers and bake for 6-10 mins., depending on oven. Watch for over-browning. Remove and immediately pour chocolate chips over hot crackers, spreading evenly as they melt. Then, top with brickle bits. Cool to room temperature then chill for at least an hour before breaking into pieces for serving.

The Sweet Potato Queens' Big-Ass Cookbook (and Financial Planner)
(Three Rivers Press, 2003), p. 151

Oh, GOD! Pie*
(AKA Coconut Caramel Pie)

Crust

1½ cups flour

1 stick salted butter, softened

1 cup finely chopped pecans

Filling

1 8-oz. pkg. cream cheese, softened

1 14-oz. can Eagle Brand® Sweetened Condensed Milk

16 ozs. CoolWhip®

Topping

1 7-oz. pkg. sweetened coconut flakes

½ stick salted butter, melted

1 cup pecan pieces

1 12-oz. jar caramel sauce

(Continues on the next page.)

Preheat oven to 350°F. In a bowl, combine flour, butter, and pecans to make two (2) pie crusts. Mash into 9″ pie pans and bake for 10 mins., until lightly browned. In a large bowl, mix together cream cheese, condensed milk, and CoolWhip®. Put into cooled pie crusts.

In a small bowl, combine coconut, butter, and pecan pieces. Spread evenly onto cookie sheet and toast it, stirring often to prevent burning. Put cooled, toasted coconut mixture on top of pies and pour caramel sauce over the tops. Chill in freezer until set.

*In many early editions of the printed books, this pie is described as CHOCOLATE caramel pie—and there is obviously NO chocolate in it. It was a typo! It is CARAMEL coconut pie. To this very day, I still get e-mails from Queens, asking, "Where's the Chocolate?" Sigh.

The Sweet Potato Queens Book of Love
(Three Rivers Press, 1999), p. 175

and

The Sweet Potato Queens' Big-Ass Cookbook (and Financial Planner)
(Three Rivers Press, 2003), p. 257

PINEAPPLE STUFF
(AKA Miss Lexie's Pineapple Casserole)

1 20-oz. can pineapple in juice, chunks or tidbits

3 TBSP juice

½ cup sugar

3 TBSP flour

1 cup Sharp Cheddar cheese, shredded

2 TBSP salted butter

½ cup Ritz® cracker crumbs

Preheat oven to 350°F. Drain pineapple and retain 3 TBSP juice. In a mixing bowl, combine juice with sugar and flour. Stir mixture into pineapple with cheese. Put into a greased, appropriate-sized baking dish. In a small sauce pan, melt butter then stir in cracker crumbs. Top pineapple with buttered crumbs then bake for 20-30 mins. Can be frozen.

The Sweet Potato Queens Book of Love
(Three Rivers Press, 1999), p. 182

and

The Sweet Potato Queens' Big-Ass Cookbook (and Financial Planner)
(Three Rivers Press, 2003), p. 258

Queen Esther's Yam Delight

Crust

1 cup flour

¼ cup powdered sugar

1/3 cup pecans, chopped

7 TBSP salted butter, softened

Preheat oven to 350°F. In a mixing bowl, combine together flour, powdered sugar, pecans, and butter. Press mixture into the bottom of a 13" x 9" x 2" pan then bake for 20 mins. Set aside to cool.

Creamy Filling

1 8-oz. pkg. cream cheese, softened

2/3 cup powdered sugar

¾ cup CoolWhip®

In a mixing bowl, combine cream cheese, powdered sugar, and CoolWhip® then spread over cooled crust.

(Continues on the next page.)

Sweet Potato Filling

1 29-oz. can sweet potatoes, drained

¼ cup sugar

¼ teaspoon cinnamon

In a mixing bowl, blend together sweet potatoes, sugar, and cinnamon. Spread over cream cheese mixture in pan.

Topping

CoolWhip®

Chopped pecans

Top with additional CoolWhip® and pecans. Chill and serve.

The Sweet Potato Queens' Field Guide to Men:
Every Man I Love is Either Married, Gay, or Dead
(Three Rivers Press, 2004), p. 226

ROCKY MOUNTAIN HIGH

2 Oreo® cookie crusts (can use pre-made)

2 sticks melted, salted butter, divided

½ cup finely chopped almonds

1 8-oz. block cream cheese

16 ozs. CoolWhip®

1 14-oz. can Eagle Brand® Sweetened Condensed Milk

7 ozs. sweetened coconut flakes

1 cup whole or sliced almonds

1 12-oz. jar caramel sauce

Preheat oven to 350°F. If using pre-made crusts, skip this first part.

To make crusts: With a kitchen mallet, smash a package of regular Oreo® cookies in a Ziploc-type bag and blend in a mixing bowl with 1 stick melted butter. Mold into 2 pie plates.

Combine ½ stick melted butter and chopped almonds and spread over the cookie crusts and pat down lightly. Bake for 10 mins. In a mixing bowl, blend together cream cheese, CoolWhip®, and condensed milk then pour into pie shells. In another bowl, mix coconut with whole or sliced almonds and ½ stick melted butter. Put the mixture on a cookie sheet and toast in oven, stirring frequently,

(Continues on the next page.)

until browned. Spread over the two pies. Slightly warm the caramel sauce to make it easier to pour and put half of it on top of each pie. Cool in the freezer only until it sets then serve.

The Sweet Potato Queens' Wedding Planner and Divorce Guide
(Crown Publishers, 2007), *Divorce Guide* side, p. 107

ROYAL TRAIL MIX

3½ cups pecan halves

¼ cup dark brown sugar

¼ cup light corn syrup

1 running-over tsp. vanilla

¼ tsp. baking soda

1½ cups dried cranberries

½ cup shredded coconut

Preheat oven to 250°F. Grease a large cookie sheet and spread pecans evenly on it. Mix together in a microwave-safe bowl brown sugar and corn syrup then microwave on *HIGH* for 1 min. Stir then microwave again for 30 seconds to 1 min., until bubbling. Stir and add vanilla and baking soda, mixing well. Drizzle mixture evenly over pecans and bake for 1 hour, stirring every 15 mins. Remove from oven and turn out onto foil-covered, rimmed, cookie sheet, spreading evenly, and allow to cool completely. Break it up into pieces, put into bowl with cranberries and coconut, mixing well.

The Sweet Potato Queens' Guide to Raising Children for Fun and Profit
(Simon & Schuster, 2008), p. 82

SISSIE MAE'S SWEET AND SALTIES

1 cup salted butter

1 cup sugar

Saltine crackers

1 10-oz. bag peanut butter chips

1 6-oz. bag chocolate chips

Preheat oven to 350°F. Line a RIMMED cookie sheet with foil then grease foil. In a small sauce pan, melt butter and sugar together, bring to a *Boil*, stir and reduce heat. Continue to cook over *LOW* heat, without stirring, for 4 mins. Arrange Saltines to cover entire foil-lined cookie sheet then pour butter mixture over them. Bake for 6 mins. Combine peanut butter chips and chocolate chips. Remove crackers from oven and pour chip mixture evenly over top, spreading as they melt. Cool to room temp then chill. Break into pieces to serve.

The Sweet Potato Queens' Big-Ass Cookbook (and Financial Planner)
(Three Rivers Press, 2003), p. 152

TCBITW's Favorite Chocolate Chip Cookies Ever*

2 cups salted butter

2 cups sugar

2 cups dark brown sugar

4 eggs

2 running-over tsp. vanilla

4 cups flour

5 cups 1-minute oatmeal

(ground *FINE* in food processor)

1 tsp. salt

2 tsp. baking soda

2 tsp. baking powder

24 ozs. Hershey's® semi-sweet chocolate chips

9 ozs. chopped plain milk chocolate Hershey® bars

3 cups chopped pecans

Preheat oven to 350°F. In a BIG-ASS mixing bowl, cream together sugars and butter, then add eggs and vanilla. Stir in remaining ingredients and mix with hands until well and evenly combined. Drop by teaspoon onto an ungreased cookie sheet. Bake 11½ minutes. (This dough freezes very well.)

*TCBITW = The Cutest Boy in the World — Jill's husband, Kyle Jennings.

This will one day appear in yet another *Sweet Potato Queens*® book, God willing.

TEXAS CORNBREAD

1 cup plain flour

1 cup self-rising flour

1 packed cup *LIGHT* brown sugar

1 cup white sugar

4 eggs

1 cup canola oil

2 cups chopped pecans

1 running-over tsp. vanilla

Preheat oven to 350°F. Mix all ingredients and pour into a greased 10" x 14" (deep sides) pan. (Size matters!) Bake for 20-25 mins.

Do NOT overcook. Should be slightly chewy.

IF you decide to share, don't use your good pan, as it will never be returned; use disposable ones.

American Thighs:
The Sweet Potato Queens' Guide to Preserving Your Assets
(Simon & Schuster, 2009), p. 299

THAT PUMPKIN STUFF THAT DOROTHY MAKES

1 16-oz. can pumpkin

1 12-oz. can evaporated milk

1 cup sugar

½ tsp. cinnamon

½ tsp. nutmeg

3 eggs

1 yellow "butter" cake mix

1 cup pecans, chopped

2 sticks salted butter, melted

Preheat oven to 350°F. Mix together in a bowl pumpkin, evaporated milk, sugar, cinnamon, nutmeg, and eggs. Pour into a greased 13" x 9" x 2" pan. Crumble cake mix and pecans on top of that and pour the melted butter over all. Bake for 50-60 mins. and cool.

(Continues on the next page.)

Frosting

8 ozs. cream cheese, softened

1 cup powdered sugar

2 cups CoolWhip®

FROSTING: In a bowl beat together with an electric handheld mixer cream cheese, powdered sugar, and CoolWhip®. Put on top of pumpkin and garnish with pecan pieces, if desired.

The Sweet Potato Queens' Big-Ass Cookbook (and Financial Planner)
(Three Rivers Press, 2003), p. 31

THE CONNER SISTERS' FAVORITE CAKE (ALSO BAILEY'S)

2¼ cups All Purpose flour

1 tsp. baking powder

1 tsp. salt

1 tsp. cinnamon

½ tsp. cloves

¼ allspice

1½ cup sugar

½ cup salted butter, softened

1 TBSP molasses

1 running over tsp. vanilla

1 scant cup milk

2 eggs

Preheat oven to 375°F. In a bowl, mix together all dry ingredients. Using an electric handheld mixer if you have one, add butter and molasses to dry ingredients. Put the vanilla in a cup with the milk and reserve ¼ cup of this mixture. Add the ¾ cup of the vanilla-milk mixture to the batter and beat until smooth. Add into this bowl, the last of the vanilla-milk mixture and the eggs. Beat again. Pour into two (2) greased and floured 9-inch cake pans. Bake for approx. 25 mins. Cool and ice with *"Browne" Sugar Frosting.* (Recipe follows.)

(Continues on the next page.)

"Browne" Sugar Frosting

½ cup salted butter

1 cup dark brown sugar

1/3 cup milk

½ tsp. vanilla

2 cups powdered sugar

In a sauce pan, melt butter. Stir in brown sugar and bring to a *Boil*. Lower heat and cook, stirring constantly, for 2 mins. Continue stirring and add milk and vanilla. Bring to *Boil* then remove from heat. Cool to lukewarm then gradually add powdered sugar, beating until smooth. (If you can't stand any lumps, sift the powdered sugar prior to use.)

This will one day appear in yet another *Sweet Potato Queens*® *book*, God willing.

THE PLUPERFECT BROWNIE

6 TBSP Hershey's® cocoa

2 sticks plus 2 TBSP salted butter

2 eggs

2 cups sugar

1 running-over tsp. vanilla

1 cup flour

¼ tsp. salt

1 cup pecans

Preheat oven to 300°F. In a sauce pan melt together cocoa and butter. In a bowl, mix eggs and sugar together and add cocoa mixture to that, then add vanilla, flour, salt, and pecans. Spread into a greased, appropriate-sized baking dish and bake for 45-50 mins.

The Sweet Potato Queens' Big-Ass Cookbook (and Financial Planner)
(Three Rivers Press, 2003), p. 58

THIRD TIME'S A CHARM

1 cup salted butter

1 cup dark brown sugar

Saltine crackers

1 12-oz. bag chocolate chips

Preheat oven to 350°F. Line a RIMMED cookie sheet with foil. In a small sauce pan, melt together butter and brown sugar. Bring that to a *Boil*, reduce heat and continue cooking on *LOW* for 4-5 mins. Cover cookie sheet with Saltines. Pour butter mixture over crackers. Bake for 6 mins. Remove from oven then pour chips over hot crackers, spreading evenly as they cool. Allow to reach room temperature then chill before serving. Break into pieces to serve.

The Sweet Potato Queens' Big-Ass Cookbook (and Financial Planner)
(Three Rivers Press, 2003), p. 153

TURTLE PIE

Crust

1½ cups Oreo® cookie crumbs

1/3 cup salted butter, melted

Filling

1¼ cups Nestlé® Toll House® Semi-sweet Chocolate Chips

1 cup evaporated milk

1 cup mini marshmallows

4 cups high-quality vanilla ice cream, softened

16 toasted pecan halves

Caramel sauce

With a kitchen mallet crush Oreos® in a Ziploc-type bag or whirl in food processor until fine crumbs. Mix with melted butter and press into deep-dish 9″ pie plate. (Ready-made chocolate pie crust may be substituted for slightly less perfect results.)

In a sauce pan, melt together chocolate chips, evaporated milk, and mini marshmallows, stirring constantly over *LOW* heat until thick and smooth. Set aside to cool.

(Continues on the next page.)

Spread soft ice cream into cooled Oreo® crust, cover and put into freezer for 30 mins. Then pour chocolate mixture over the ice cream, cover and return to freezer for additional 30 mins.

Remove from freezer and add additional 2 cups ice cream, cover with remaining chocolate mixture; return to freezer again for 30 mins. Remove from freezer, lightly press toasted pecan halves into top chocolate layer.

Serve with caramel sauce in quantity to personal preference.

The Sweet Potato Queens' Field Guide to Men:
Every Man I Love is Either Married, Gay, or Dead
(Three Rivers Press, 2004), p. 228

TWINKIE® PIE

Hostess Twinkies®
Instant vanilla pudding
Sliced fruit of choice

Cut Twinkies® in half, lengthwise and line a pan (sized to your appetite) with them. (This is a very flexible recipe, quantities easily adjustable.) Prepare pudding according to package directions and spread over Twinkies®. Top with sliced bananas, strawberries, peaches, etc. You may even use drained fruit cocktail, if no fresh fruit is available.

God Save the Sweet Potato Queens
(Three Rivers Press, 2001), p. 224

and

The Sweet Potato Queens' Big-Ass Cookbook (and Financial Planner)
(Three Rivers Press, 2003), p. 263

VINEY'S CARAMEL PECAN PIE

1 9" pie shell, unbaked

36 caramels, unwrapped

¼ cup salted butter

¼ cup milk

¾ cup sugar

3 eggs

½ tsp. vanilla

¼ tsp. salt

1 cup pecan halves

Preheat oven to 350°F. Combine caramels, butter, and milk in a sauce pan and cook over *LOW* heat, stirring frequently, until smooth. Remove from heat and set aside. In a large bowl, combine sugar, eggs, vanilla, and salt. Gradually stir in the caramel mixture. Stir in pecans. Pour into unbaked pie shell in a 9" pie pan. Bake for 45-50 mins. or until pastry is golden brown. Cool to allow filling to set before serving.

This will one day appear in yet another *Sweet Potato Queens® book*, God willing.

WET BROWNIES ICE CREAM

12 egg yolks

6 cups whole milk

4 cups sugar

1-1/3 cups Hershey's® cocoa

8 cups Half & Half

4 running over tsp. vanilla

Mix egg yolks, milk, and sugar in large pot. Cook, stirring constantly, until it thickens enough to coat the spoon. Remove from heat and sift in cocoa. With an electric handheld mixer, beat until smooth and creamy. Allow to cool then add Half & Half and vanilla. Refrigerate overnight if possible before putting into an electric ice cream maker.

The Sweet Potato Queens' Guide to Raising Children for Fun and Profit
(Simon & Schuster, 2008), p. 77

WHO NEEDS HIM? NANNER PUDDIN'

1 large pkg. instant banana pudding mix

1/3 cup CoffeeMate®
(Original or French Vanilla)

2½ cups milk

1 14-oz. can Eagle Brand® Sweetened Condensed Milk

1 12-oz. tub Extra Creamy Cool-Whip®

Vanilla wafers

Sliced bananas

In a mixing bowl, combine pudding mix with CoffeeMate®, milk, condensed milk, and Cool-Whip®. Line an appropriate-sized serving dish or compote with vanilla wafers and sliced bananas. Put a layer of the pudding mix on top. Repeat layers.

The Sweet Potato Queens' Wedding Planner and Divorce Guide
(Crown Publishers, 2007), *Divorce Guide* side, p. 119

YAM YOMP

Crust & Topping

3 cups quick oats (*never Instant*)

3 cups flour

4½ cups dark brown sugar

2 tsp. cinnamon

½ tsp. salt

1½ lbs. salted butter, softened

Preheat oven to 350°F. Mix all together. Put ¼ of the mixture into each of two (2) greased 13" x 9" x 2" pans, mashing to cover sides and bottom of pans. Bake for 10 mins.

Filling

4 eggs

4 cups sweet potatoes, mashed (may use canned)

1 14-oz. cans sweetened, condensed milk

¼ tsp. salt

Caramel sauce, optional

(Continues on the next page.)

With an electric handheld mixer, beat eggs, add sweet potatoes, condensed milk, and salt. Pour into crusts and top with remaining oatmeal mixture. Bake for about 50 mins. Cover loosely with foil if necessary to prevent over-browning in final mins. Serve warm with ice cream and caramel sauce (if desired).

The Sweet Potato Queens' Big-Ass Cookbook (and Financial Planner)
(Three Rivers Press, 2003), p. 238

YES, IT'S ONE MORE DUMP CAKE VARIATION
(AKA Apple Crack)

2 cans apple pie filling

2 sticks salted butter, melted

1 box yellow cake mix

1 cup dark brown sugar

1 tsp. cinnamon

2 cups pecan pieces

Preheat oven to 350°F. Spread pie filling into a 13" x 9" x 2" pan, sprayed with Pam®. Mix together melted butter, cake mix, brown sugar, cinnamon, and pecans. Spread evenly over pie filling. Bake for 40-45 mins. until brown and crispy on top. (Watch pecans for over-browning, cover pan loosely with foil if necessary.)

The Sweet Potato Queens' Guide to Raising Children for Fun and Profit
(Simon & Schuster, 2008), p. 86

VEGGIES

Boys 'r' Us Beans

1 stick salted butter

¾ cup dark brown sugar

1 TBSP soy sauce

1 tsp. chopped garlic

2 14.5-oz. cans green beans, drained

Crisp bacon

Preheat oven to 300°F. In a sauce pan, melt butter, sugar, soy, and garlic together. Add beans and stir well. Put into an appropriate-sized baking dish, top with liberal amount of crisp bacon. Cover and bake for 45 mins.

The Sweet Potato Queens' First Big-Ass Novel:
Stuff we didn't actually do, but could have, and may yet
(Simon & Schuster, 2008), p. 282

CARROTS A KID COULD LOVE

1 lb. carrots, split lengthwise

½ stick salted butter

1-2 TBSP lemon juice

2 TBSP dark brown sugar

In a sauce pan, cook carrots in lightly salted water until tender. Drain well. Melt butter and add juice and sugar; cook, stirring, until it thickens. Pour over carrots then toss until well-coated.

The Sweet Potato Queens' Guide to Raising Children for Fun and Profit
(Simon & Schuster, 2008), p. 80

CONNIE'S DEATH CORN FIVE
(AKA Death Corn Five)

1 pkg. Zatarain's® yellow rice,

cooked according to directions, omit oil

1 11-oz. can Green Giant® SteamCrisp® Mexicorn®

1 10.5-oz. can cream of chicken soup

1 stick salted butter, melted

1 cup Sharp Cheddar or Pepper Jack cheese, shredded

Preheat oven to 350°F. In a mixing bowl, combine cooked rice with all other ingredients. Put into an appropriate-sized baking dish and bake for 20 mins. or until bubbly.

God Save the Sweet Potato Queens
(Three Rivers Press, 2001), p. 215

and

The Sweet Potato Queens' Big-Ass Cookbook (and Financial Planner)
(Three Rivers Press, 2003), p. 259

CORN AND BEANS AND 'MATERS AND BACON

1 medium onion, chopped

1 green pepper, chopped

3-4 TBSP olive oil

1 16-oz. can whole-kernel white corn, drained

1 17-oz. can lima beans, drained

1 8-oz. can tomato sauce

1 16-oz. can stewed tomatoes

1 TBSP Worcestershire sauce

Salt and pepper to taste

Bacon, uncooked

Preheat oven to 350°F. In an iron skillet with a lid or stainless steel skillet with an oven-safe lid, cook onion and pepper in oil until tender. Combine in the skillet or pan corn, limas, sauce, tomatoes, Worcestershire, salt, and pepper. Top with strips of bacon. Bake, covered, for 50 mins., then uncover and cook for 10 more mins. to crisp bacon.

The Sweet Potato Queens' Big-Ass Cookbook (and Financial Planner)
(Three Rivers Press, 2003), p. 229

CORN AND PEPPERS WITH ENHANCED FAT CONTENT

2 TBSP olive oil

2 fresh Poblano or Anaheim peppers, seeded and chopped

1 small onion, chopped fine

1 clove garlic, chopped

1 10-oz. pkg. frozen corn

½ cup light cream

2 TBSP cilantro, chopped fine

½ tsp. salt

In an iron skillet or a stainless steel skillet, cook peppers, onion, and garlic in oil until tender. Add all other ingredients and cook over *MEDIUM* heat until cream is slightly thickened.

The Sweet Potato Queens' Big-Ass Cookbook (and Financial Planner)
(Three Rivers Press, 2003), p. 226

CRAZY-GOOD CABBAGE

1 small cabbage, cut up

1 medium Vidalia (or other sweet) onion, chopped

1 10.5-oz. can cream of chicken soup*

1 cup mayo

½ stick salted butter, melted

Topping

1 stick salted butter, melted

1 cup Sharp Cheddar cheese, shredded

1 sleeve Ritz® crackers, crushed

Preheat oven to 350°F. Grease a 13″ x 9″ x 2″ baking dish. Put chopped cabbage in dish, top with chopped onions. In a bowl, mix together soup, mayo, and butter. Pour over vegetables.

In a bowl, mix together butter, cheese, and cracker crumbs. Spread over top of everything in the baking dish. Bake approx. 45 mins.

*If you prefer not to use canned soup, you may substitute a scratch-made…

(Continues on next page.)

Béchamel Sauce

½ cup chicken broth

½ cup milk

3 TBSP butter

3 TBSP flour

Salt and pepper to taste

Melt butter and flour together in a small sauce pan, stirring constantly. Slowly add in broth and milk while bringing to a *Gentle Boil* and cooking until desired thickness is reached.

This will one day appear in yet another *Sweet Potato Queens® book*, God willing.

DEATH CORN FIVE
(AKA Connie's Death Corn Five)

1 pkg. Zatarain's® yellow rice,
cooked according to directions, omit oil

1 11-oz. can Green Giant® SteamCrisp® Mexicorn®

1 10.5-oz. can cream of chicken soup

1 stick salted butter, melted

1 cup Sharp Cheddar or Pepper Jack cheese, shredded

Preheat oven to 350°F. In a mixing bowl, combine cooked rice with all other ingredients. Put into an appropriate-sized baking dish and bake for 20 mins. or until bubbly.

God Save the Sweet Potato Queens
(Three Rivers Press, 2001), p. 215

and

The Sweet Potato Queens' Big-Ass Cookbook (and Financial Planner)
(Three Rivers Press, 2003), p. 259

Enchanting Enchiladas

3-4 lbs. Yellow or Zucchini squash, cut up

1 large onion, chopped

¼ tsp. minced garlic

3-4 TBSP olive oil

2 4-oz. cans chopped green chilis

Heat oil in large skillet, add onions and garlic, cook until tender. Add squash, cover then cook until tender. Stir in chilis and set aside.

(Continues on the next page.)

Sauce

4 TBSP salted butter

4 TBSP flour

4 tsp. chili powder

½ tsp. salt

2 cups milk

2-3 cups Pepper Jack or Sharp Cheddar cheese, shredded

1 15-oz. can diced tomatoes, drained

Flour tortillas, warmed

FOR SAUCE: in a small sauce pan, melt butter, stir in flour until smooth. Add chili powder, salt, and milk. Cook over *MEDIUM* heat until it begins to thicken, then add cheese. Cook, stirring, until melted and smooth. Add sauce to squash until desired consistency. Stir in tomatoes until heated through. (Extra sauce will freeze.) Serve in warm tortillas — *it's very messy.*

The Sweet Potato Queens' Big-Ass Cookbook (and Financial Planner)
(Three Rivers Press, 2003), p. 188

EVEN BAILEY WILL EAT THIS SQUASH

3-4 lbs. Yellow or Zucchini squash

1 medium onion, chopped

2 cups Sharp Cheddar cheese, shredded

2 egg whites, beaten

1-2 sleeves Saltine crackers, crushed

Salted butter, melted

Preheat oven to 350°F. In a large sauce pan, *Boil* squash and onions until tender. Drain. Mash with potato masher and add cheese. Fold in egg whites. Put into a greased, appropriate-sized baking dish and top with Saltine crumbs and melted butter. Bake until bubbly around edges.

The Sweet Potato Queens' Guide to Raising Children for Fun and Profit
(Simon & Schuster, 2008), p. 79

FANCY TATERS

5 TBSP salted butter, divided

1 clove garlic, minced

2½ lbs. Yukon Gold potatoes, peeled, sliced thin

1 tsp. salt, divided

1 tsp. white pepper, divided

1 cup Gruyère cheese, grated

1¼ cup whipping cream

1 TBSP flour

Preheat oven to 400°F. Mix 1 TBSP butter with garlic and rub inside of a 2½ quart casserole with it. Put half of the potatoes in the dish and sprinkle with ½ tsp. salt and ½ tsp. white pepper. Put 2 TBSP butter, cut in pieces, on top of potatoes and top with ½ cup cheese. Repeat all for another layer. Mix whipping cream and flour in a small sauce pan; cook over *MEDIUM* heat (*do not boil*), stirring until smooth. Pour over potatoes; cover, then bake for 20 mins.; uncover, then bake for another 30-40 mins.

The Sweet Potato Queens' Big-Ass Cookbook (and Financial Planner)
(Three Rivers Press, 2003), p. 165

GREAT GOUDA GOODNESS

2 TBSP salted butter

1 large Vidalia onion, sliced into thin rounds

Garlic to taste

1/8 cup water

1 cup heavy cream

½ cup cottage cheese

1 tsp. salt

1 cup Parmesan

2 large zucchini, sliced into ¼ inch rounds

2 large yellow squash, sliced ¼ inch rounds

½ cup crisp bacon (optional)

1½ cups smoked Gouda, grated

Preheat oven to 400°F. Melt butter in an iron skillet or stainless steel skillet with an oven-safe handle. Add onion then cook until translucent. Add garlic and cook 2-3 mins. Add squash and water. Stir then cover. Cook just until squash softens. Uncover and cook until water is gone. (If too much liquid, slide squash to one side of pan, wad up paper towels and just sop it up.) Mix cream and cottage cheese together then stir into squash. Cook, stirring, until it begins to thicken slightly. Stir in Parmesan and salt. Remove from heat then top with bacon (if using) and spread Gouda over the top. Bake for 20 mins. or until cheese is brown. Let stand several mins. before serving.

This will one day appear in yet another *Sweet Potato Queens*® *book*, God willing.

LARRUPIN' GOOD SWEET POTATOES

3 cups cooked sweet potatoes

1 cup sugar

1/3 cup milk

1 stick salted butter

1 running-over teaspoon vanilla

2 eggs, beaten

Dash salt

Preheat oven to 350°F. With a potato masher, mash together in a mixing bowl potatoes, sugar, milk, butter, vanilla, and salt. Taste for desired sweetness before adding eggs. Add sugar if needed, then add eggs and mix well. Put into a greased, appropriate-sized baking dish.

(Continues on the next page.)

.

Topping

1 cup dark brown sugar

1/3 cup salted butter

1/3 cup flour

1 cup pecan pieces

1 cup coconut (optional)

In a mixing bowl, blend together brown sugar, butter, flour, pecans (and coconut, if desired). Spread over top of potatoes then bake for about 30 mins. Watch for over-browning.

God Save the Sweet Potato Queens
(Three Rivers Press, 2001), p. 217

and

The Sweet Potato Queens' Big-Ass Cookbook (and Financial Planner)
(Three Rivers Press, 2003), p. 260

LAWYERLY TATERS

3-5 lbs. peeled potatoes

1 8-oz. carton sour cream

2 bunches green onions, chopped

2 cups Cheddar cheese, shredded

Preheat oven to 300°F. In a large stock pot, *Boil* potatoes until soft, drain and put into a LARGE baking dish. In a small sauce pan, melt together sour cream, onions, and cheese. Pour over potatoes, stirring to coat evenly. Bake for 20 mins. Remove from oven and sprinkle with a bit more cheese.

The Sweet Potato Queens' Big-Ass Cookbook (and Financial Planner)
(Three Rivers Press, 2003), p. 221

LOVE-APPLE (TOMATO) PIE
(regular or crustless)

5 medium tomatoes, skinned, chopped into chunks

1 medium onion, chopped

½ clove garlic

1 TBSP dark brown sugar

2 TBSP chopped basil (fresh or freeze-dried)

Salt to taste

1 cup shredded Swiss cheese

1 cup shredded Sharp Cheddar cheese

¾ cup mayo

1 baked 10″ pie shell (cooled) — OPTIONAL

Preheat oven to 400°F. Peel and chop tomatoes. Mix all ingredients, except pie shell, then bake in a greased 13″ x 9″ x 2″ pan for 20-25 mins.; or, spoon into pie crust and bake. Let stand for several minutes after baking.

This will one day appear in yet another *Sweet Potato Queens®* book, God willing.

MAKE-BELIEVE-YOU-CAN-COOK PEGLEG CORN

1 stick salted butter

1 8-oz. block cream cheese

2 11-oz. cans white Shoepeg corn, drained

¼ cup diced jalapeños

Cooked bacon, optional

Preheat oven to 350°F. In a small sauce pan, melt butter and cream cheese together, add corn and peppers. Put into an appropriate-sized baking dish then bake until bubbly. Also, it is good with crumbled bacon added…of course.

Fat Is The New 30:
The Sweet Potato Queens' Guide to Coping with (the crappy parts of) Life
(Amazon Publishing, 2012), p. 141

My Next Husband's Grilled Sweet Potatoes
(Used by permission from Robert St. John: *New South Grilling*)

4 sweet potatoes, peeled

½ cup salted butter, softened

2 TBSP dark brown sugar

¼ tsp. cinnamon

1 tsp. hot sauce

Kosher salt

Black pepper

In a mixing bowl, combine butter, sugar, cinnamon, and hot sauce. Cut potatoes into ½" thick slices then put onto cookie sheet and brush with butter mixture. Place them on the grill, direct *MEDIUM* heat, buttered side down. Brush tops with more butter mixture. Cook for 12-15 mins., until tender, turning once. Remove from grill, brush with any remaining butter and sprinkle with Kosher salt and pepper to taste.

American Thighs:
The Sweet Potato Queens' Guide to Preserving Your Assets
(Simon & Schuster, 2009), p. 295

PRALINE SWEET POTATOES

6 lbs. cooked sweet potatoes,
peeled & mashed (may use canned)

2 sticks salted butter, softened

2 TBSP dark brown sugar

1 TBSP Steen's® Louisiana Cane Syrup

1/3 cup Eagle Brand® Sweetened Condensed Milk

1/8 tsp. ground nutmeg

¼ tsp. cinnamon sugar

1 tsp. lemon juice

Zest of 1 lemon

1 TBSP orange juice

1 cup raisins

2 cups chopped pecans

8 ozs. Classic, New Orleans Famous Pralines®, crumbled

Meringue (optional)

Preheat oven to 350°F. In a BIG-ASS mixing bowl, stir together potatoes (peeled after cooking), butter, sugar, syrup, milk, and spices—blend well. Add juices and zest. Then, gently add raisins, pecans, and praline crumbles. Bake in foil-covered large casserole for 45 mins. If desired, remove and cool slightly before topping with meringue and browning in oven.

The Sweet Potato Queens' Big-Ass Cookbook (and Financial Planner)
(Three Rivers Press, 2003), p. 168

Spinach Madeline

2 bags (20 – 24 ozs.) frozen chopped or cut leaf spinach

4 TBSP salted butter

2 TBSP flour

2 TBSP onion, chopped

Velveeta® Jalapeño cheese (*Important note below), cut into small chunks

½ cup evaporated milk

½ cup "vegetable liquor"

¾ tsp. celery salt

¾ tsp. garlic salt

Cayenne pepper to taste

1 TBSP Worcestershire sauce

1 sleeve Ritz® crackers (optional)

3 TBSP salted butter, melted (optional)

Cook spinach in sauce pan with 2 cups water. Drain but reserve ½ cup of the liquid ("vegetable liquor"). In another medium sauce pan, melt butter over *LOW* heat, add flour, stirring until blended and smooth. Slowly add reserved "vegetable liquor", stirring constantly. Add evaporated milk and cook, stirring, until it begins to thicken. Add seasonings and Velveeta®; continue cooking, stirring until all is melted. Stir in spinach. May serve immediately.

(Continues on the next page.)

For best flavor: put into a greased 1½ qt. casserole dish, let cool, cover, then refrigerate overnight. Top with buttered Ritz® crumbs (combine crushed crackers with 3 TBSP melted butter) and bake at 350°F, until bubbly.

* Velveeta® Jalapeño is not available everywhere. May use plain Velveeta® and add 2-3 TBSP diced jalapeño or to taste.

HIGHLY recommend doubling this recipe.

This will one day appear in yet another *Sweet Potato Queens® book*, God willing.

SYLVIA'S STOVELESS BLACK BEANS

2 lbs. smoked turkey necks, wings, or drums

2 16-oz. pkgs. dried black beans

1 large onion, chopped fine

2 bay leaves

Crushed red pepper

Sylvia's Secret Seasoning®

Water

Nacho Cheese Doritos®

Original "Louisiana" Brand® Hot Sauce

Put beans into a large stock pot, cover with water and bring to a *Rolling Boil*. Then turn off and allow to sit for 1 hour. Rinse beans and put into Crock-Pot® with turkey, onions, bay leaves, red pepper, and Sylvia's Secret Seasoning®. Cover with water and cook on *HIGH* for 2 hours; then, reduce to *LOW* and cook for 24 hours. Remove and discard turkey bones and bay leaves. Serve beans with Original "Louisiana" Brand® Hot Sauce and Doritos®.

The Sweet Potato Queens' Big-Ass Cookbook (and Financial Planner)
(Three Rivers Press, 2003), p. 234

WHIRLED PEAS

1 stick salted butter

Thin-sliced carrots

English (green) peas, fresh or frozen

Fresh dill, chopped (may substitute dried)

Melt butter in heavy skillet and cook carrot slices until tender. (May steam briefly in microwave first if in a hurry or if slices are thicker.) Add peas, cook until tender then add dill. Stir well to coat, cooking a few more mins.

The Sweet Potato Queens' Field Guide to Men:
Every Man I Love is Either Married, Gay, or Dead
(Three Rivers Press, 2004), p. 222

WEIRD SHIT

CHRISTMAS SALAD

1 large bag Golden Flake® Hot Chips

1 large bag Golden Flake® Pickle Chips

Empty both bags into a large bowl and toss lightly.

The Sweet Potato Queens' Wedding Planner and Divorce Guide
(Crown Publishers, 2007), *Divorce Guide* side, p. 118

DAMON LEE FOWLER'S BACON POPCORN
(Damon Lee Fowler's Recipe; used with permission.)

Real popcorn (NOT microwave)

Vegetable oil

3 TBSP bacon grease, hot

Salt

In a large stock pot with a lid, heat oil and pop the popcorn. Put hot popcorn into a paper bag, drizzle hot bacon grease over popcorn, hold bag closed and shake. Salt to taste and shake bag again.

The Sweet Potato Queens' First Big-Ass Novel:
Stuff we didn't actually do, but could have, and may yet
(Simon & Schuster, 2008), p. 288

FRIED DILL PICKLES, BY GEORGE

1 cup self-rising flour

1 tsp. baking powder

¼ tsp. paprika

1/8 tsp. red pepper

1/3 cup Corona® beer

1/3 cup milk

Dill pickle slices

Oil for frying

Sift together in a flour, baking powder, paprika, and red pepper. Add beer and milk. Dip pickle slices in batter and drop into deep, hot oil in a large pot. (Don't crowd it.) Fry until evenly brown. Salt to taste.

The Sweet Potato Queens' Big-Ass Cookbook (and Financial Planner)
(Three Rivers Press, 2003), p. 213

FRIED NOODLES

Extra wide egg noodles,
prepared according to package
Salted butter
Kosher salt
Crushed red pepper (optional)

Melt butter in heavy skillet so bottom is covered. Dump in cooked noodles, mash with spatula and fry, turning as needed, until golden brown and crispy. Add butter as needed or desired. Sprinkle with Kosher salt and red pepper. (Any spice you like may be used.)

The Sweet Potato Queens' Guide to Raising Children for Fun and Profit
(Simon & Schuster, 2008), p. 83

HEALTH-NUT FAMILY'S FAMOUS FRIED APPLES

Jonathan apples, sliced thin (peeling optional)

Bacon, cut into tiny pieces

Sugar (white or dark brown)

In a skillet with a lid, fry bacon bits until nearly done then add apple slices, cover and cook, stirring occasionally, until apples are translucent. Add sugar (amount optional, depending on number of apples used — start with at least 2 TBSP per apple used, add more if desired.) Cook, covered but stirring frequently, until sugar begins to caramelize. Serve over warm bread or ice cream.

American Thighs:
The Sweet Potato Queens' Guide to Preserving Your Assets
(Simon & Schuster, 2009), p. 291

LINDA'S PERKY PICKLES

1 gal. dill pickles, drained; juice reserved

Sugar

1 jar jalapeños (optional)

Slice up pickles according to preference—chips or wedges. Put into four (4) 1-quart jars. Allow 1 cup pickle juice per quart jar. First, put juice into a large pot and add 1-1/3 cup sugar per cup of pickle juice. Heat until sugar is dissolved. Add jalapeños and/or jalapeños juice to taste. Then, pour this "new" juice over pickles in the jars; cap the jars and keep refrigerated.

The Sweet Potato Queens' Big-Ass Cookbook (and Financial Planner)
(Three Rivers Press, 2003), p. 28

LOVE LARD

1 lb. bacon

1 loaf white bread

1 can cream of mushroom soup

Preheat oven to 325°F. Trim crusts from bread and cut each slice into thirds. Smear each slice with soup and place one bacon strip on top. Roll up and secure with a toothpick then place on a rimmed cookie sheet. Bake for one hour.

The Sweet Potato Queens' Big-Ass Cookbook (and Financial Planner)
(Three Rivers Press, 2003), p. 161

RACCOON LOAF

1 lb. bulk pork sausage, hot

1 small chopped onion

2 canned ("whomp") pizza crusts

Monterey Jack cheese

Jalapeño slices

Preheat oven to 350°F. In a skillet, brown sausage and onions then drain off fat. On an ungreased cookie sheet, spread out the raw pizza crusts, top with cheese (amount optional), half the sausage/onion mixture, and jalapeños (amount optional). Roll up and pinch ends together as you go. Bake for 10 mins. or until dough is done. Slice and eat or freeze for later.

The Sweet Potato Queens' Wedding Planner and Divorce Guide
(Crown Publishers, 2007), *Divorce Guide* side, p. 117

SNEAKY TREATS

1 tsp. vanilla

1 8-oz. pkg. cream cheese, softened (may use low-fat)

½ cup crushed pineapple, drained

1 cup sugar (or Splenda®)

2 tsp. cinnamon

1 stick salted butter, melted

18 slices white bread, crusts removed

Preheat oven to 350°F. In a mixing bowl, blend together the vanilla, cream cheese, and pineapple. In another bowl, combine sugar and cinnamon. Spread pineapple mixture on bread slices, fold two sides of bread to the middle. Brush with melted butter and roll in cinnamon/sugar mix. Bake on cookie sheet for 15-20 mins.

The Sweet Potato Queens' Guide to Raising Children for Fun and Profit
(Simon & Schuster, 2008), p. 84

RECOMMENDATIONS *

You can easily purchase online all of the various accoutrements referenced within the pages of this book by buying the electronic version too. (I use the Kindle App on my phone for this e-Book to give me the ingredients while shopping and I use the print version while cooking. But that's just me.) At any rate, the e-Book has active hyperlinks to everything at Amazon, provided you're not reading it on an Apple product. If you use Apple products to consume e-Books or you only have this printed copy, then go online at www.SweetPotatoQueens.com/Recommendations to access all of the following items.

APPLIANCES

Blender, Ninja® Countertop

Food Processor (selection), Cuisinart® Collection

Handheld Electric Mixer, Cuisinart®

Ice Cream Maker, electric

Instant Pot®

Slow Cooker, Crock-Pot®, 6-qt.

BOOKS BY JILL CONNER BROWNE

Fat Is The New 30:
The Sweet Potato Queens' Guide to Coping with (the crappy parts of) Life
(Amazon Publishing, 2012)

American Thighs:
The Sweet Potato Queens' Guide to Preserving Your Assets
(Simon & Schuster, 2009)

The Sweet Potato Queens' Guide to Raising Children for Fun and Profit
(Simon & Schuster, 2008)

The Sweet Potato Queens' First Big-Ass Novel:
Stuff we didn't actually do, but could have, and may yet
(Simon & Schuster, 2008)

The Sweet Potato Queens' Wedding Planner and Divorce Guide
(Crown Publishers, 2007)

The Sweet Potato Queens' Field Guide to Men:
Every Man I Love is Either Married, Gay, or Dead
(Three Rivers Press, 2004)

The Sweet Potato Queens' Big-Ass Cookbook (and Financial Planner)
(Three Rivers Press, 2003)

God Save the Sweet Potato Queens
(Three Rivers Press, 2001)

The Sweet Potato Queens Book of Love
(Three Rivers Press, 1999)

BOOKS BY OTHER AUTHORS

Deep South Staples:
or How to Survive in a Southern Kitchen
Without a Can of Cream of Mushroom Soup
(St. John, Robert; Hyperion 2006)

New South Grilling:
Fresh and Exciting Recipes from the Third Coast
(St. John, Robert; Hyperion 2008)

Robert's other titles are available at your favorite bookseller.

and

Damon Lee Fowler's books are available at your favorite bookseller.

BAKING / SERVING DISHES

CorningWare® Bakeware

Demitasse Cups

Pyrex® Baking Dish, 2-qt. Oblong

Pyrex® Baking Dish, 4.8-qt. (10" x 15" x 2")

Pyrex® Deep Baking Dish Set

Pyrex® 9.5" Pie Plate

Ramekins, small

BOWLS

Nordic Ware® Mixing Bowl Set w/Lids

Pyrex® Mixing Bowl Set w/Lids

Tupperware® Mixing Bowl, BIG-ASS (32-cups)

Pyrex® Storage Bowl Set (prep, microwave/preheated oven-safe)

GROCERIES (Only those items not available everywhere.)

Grissini Breadsticks, three (3), 3-oz. boxes

Manischewitz® Matzo Meal

McClard's® Bar-B-Q Sauce

Quick Grits

Steen's® Louisiana Cane Syrup

Sylvia's Secret Seasoning®

KITCHEN & BAR UTENSILS

Bread Knife

Candy Thermometer

Cocktail Shaker, shatterproof

Drinkware, stemless, suitable for outdoor use

Glasses, Martini

Food Prep Surfaces (selection)

Food Prep Gloves, disposable

Graters and Zesters (selection)

Kitchen Mallet

Measuring Spoons

Measuring Cups

Melon Baller

Pastry Basting Brush

Peel, Pare, and Slice Set

Pitcher, large, w/margarita glasses

Pitcher, sealable

Potato Masher

Sealable Container, large

Serving Spatula

Sifter

Whisk

Wooden Spoon

KITCHEN CONSUMABLES

Aluminum Foil, *HEAVY*

Aluminum Foil, Non-Stick

Aluminum Pans, 10" x 14", disposable

Bamboo Skewer

Canning Jar, 16 oz.

1-quart jars, four (4)

Matches, long

Parchment Paper

Plastic Wrap

Wax Paper

MISCELLANEOUS

Charcoal Grill (Weber® Original Kettle Premium)

Double Boiler, covered, 2-qt.

Gooseneck Phone/Pad/Tablet Holders

Grill Basket, closed

Grill Basket, open

Microwave-safe Mug

Microwave Steaming Container

PANS / SHEETS

Baking Pan, 8" x 8" x 2"

Baking Pan, 8" square, layer pan w/handles

Baking Pan, 13" x 9" x 2"

Baking Pan, 13" x 9" x 2", commercial grade w/lid

Baking Pan, 10" x 14" (deep sides), commercial grade

Baking Pan, extra-large (20.25" x 14.25" x 1") w/cooling rack

Broiler Pan

Bundt Pans (size and style selection)

Bundt Pan, 12-cup w/handles

Cookie Sheets and Sheet Pans, rimmed (size and style selection)

Cupcake and Muffin Pans (size and style selection)

Loaf Pan

Loaf Pan, mini (8 wells)

Muffin Pan, 12 cups

Muffin Pan, mini

Muffin Pan, Texas-sized

Pie Pan, 9" commercial grade w/handles

Pie Pan, 9" deep-dish

Sheet Baking Pan, large, high-sided (17.75" x 13" x 2")

Sheet Baking Pan, mini (9" x 6" x 1"), fits most toaster ovens

SAUCE PANS / POTS

Sauce Pan w/lid, Large (4-qt.)

Sauce Pan w/lid, Medium (3-qt.)

Sauce Pan w/lid, Small (1.5 qt.)

Stock Pot w/lid, Large (8-qt)

SKILLETS/FRYING PANS

Iron Skillet, 12-inch

Iron Skillet w/lid, DEEP (5-qt.)

Stainless Steel Skillet, 10.5" w/Oven-safe Lid

Stainless Steel Skillet, Large, 12"

Stainless Steel Frying Pans (size selection)

* LIMITS OF LIABILITY AND DISCLAIMER OF WARRANTY: THE AUTHOR AND PUBLISHER OF THIS BOOK, SPQ, INC. AND SWEET POTATO QUEENS WEBSITE, LLC. HAVE USED THEIR BEST EFFORTS IN PREPARING THIS MATERIAL. THE AUTHOR AND PUBLISHER MAKE NO REPRESENTATIONS OR WARRANTIES WITH RESPECT TO THE ACCURACY, APPLICABILITY, FITNESS OR COMPLETENESS OF THE CONTENTS OF THIS MATERIAL. THEY DISCLAIM ANY WARRANTIES EXPRESSED OR IMPLIED, MERCHANTABILITY, OR FITNESS FOR ANY PARTICULAR PURPOSE. THE AUTHOR AND PUBLISHER SHALL IN NO EVENT BE HELD LIABLE FOR ANY LOSS OR OTHER DAMAGES, INCLUDING BUT NOT LIMITED TO, SPECIAL, INCIDENTAL, CONSEQUENTIAL, OR OTHER DAMAGES. THIS MATERIAL CONTAINS ELEMENTS PROTECTED UNDER INTERNATIONAL AND FEDERAL COPYRIGHT AND TRADEMARK LAWS AND TREATIES. ANY UNAUTHORIZED REPRINT OR USE OF THIS MATERIAL IS PROHIBITED.

HYPERLINKS: SWEET POTATO QUEENS WEBSITE, LLC. IS A PARTICIPANT IN THE AMAZON SERVICES LLC. ASSOCIATES PROGRAM, AN AFFILIATE ADVERTISING PROGRAM DESIGNED TO PROVIDE A MEANS FOR IT TO EARN FEES BY LINKING TO AMAZON.COM AND AFFILIATED SITES.

Made in the USA
Monee, IL
23 September 2022

14505693R00188